MILITARY WIDOW

MILITARY WIDOW

A Survival Guide

by

Joanne M. Steen and M. Regina Asaro

NAVAL INSTITUTE PRESS

ANNAPOLIS, MARYLAND

Naval Institute Press
291 Wood Road
Annapolis, MD 21402

ISBN-13: 978-1-59114-834-0

Library of Congress Cataloging-in-Publication Data
Steen, Joanne M.
Military widow : a survival guide / by Joanne M. Steen, M. Regina Asaro.
    p. cm.
Includes bibliographical references.
ISBN 1-59114-834-0 (alk. paper)
1. War widows—Services for—United States. 2. War widows—United States—
Psychology. 3. Grief therapy. 4. Military spouses—United States. I. Asaro, M.
Regina. II. Title.
  UB403.S74 2006
  155.9'3708654—dc22

                        2006007366

Printed in the United States of America on acid-free paper ∞
13 12 11 10 09 08 07   9 8 7 6 5 4 3

"I hope I've made you proud
of the way I've faced the future,
and carried on without you.
Until we meet again,
Goodnight, My Love."

CONTENTS

PREFACE

WHEN MY HUSBAND, KEN, WAS KILLED in the line of duty, I (Joanne) was shocked to learn that no grief book existed that addressed military widowhood. There were plenty of books on grief, but few addressed the needs of the young widow, and none focused solely on the military widow. I had to rely on other military widows for advice, help, and encouragement.

Six years later, while providing support to new military widows, I realized they were struggling with the same issues I had faced years earlier. This revelation sparked the idea for a survival guide for the military widow.

While responding to an Air National Guard aviation mishap in March 2001, I met Regina Asaro, a fellow crisis responder and a psychiatric nurse. Regina also knew that few written resources existed for the military widow. Together, we made the commitment to write a survival guide that would address the specific needs of a military widow. As military spouses, we knew we possessed the necessary insight into the culture of the military and could quickly identify the unique needs and issues that confront military widows as they struggle to cope with their life-changing loss.

Between us, we have many years of experience facilitating grief support groups for young military widows and homicide survivors, and extensive experience as crisis responders in the military and civilian sectors. We have relied on our personal and professional experiences with grief and traumatic loss, as well as the following sources, in preparing *Military Widow: A Survival Guide*:

- in-depth interviews with military widows;
- briefings with casualty officers, chaplains, and command leaders;
- discussions with active duty and retired military personnel;
- research on grief, traumatic loss, and posttraumatic stress disorder; and

- presentations on the topics of traumatic loss, crisis intervention, and military grief to mental health professionals, casualty assistance officers, military chaplains, and military family survivors.

As a result of these efforts, we were able to write *Military Widow: A Survival Guide*. It is the first book of its kind, one that tackles the tough subject of military widowhood with compassion, empathy, knowledge, and experience. Our hopes for the book are twofold: that it will help every military widow to better understand her emotions, actions, and thoughts, and that it will give her family, friends, and the military personnel who support her a better idea of what she is experiencing.

ACKNOWLEDGMENTS

OUR BOOK COULD NOT HAVE BEEN WRITTEN without the help of many fine people. First and foremost, we thank the many military widows who, in the midst of their personal tragedy, reached out to help us help the newest widows to walk an easier road.

We also thank the men and women of our armed forces who selflessly gave their time, energy, and talent to aid the widows of their fallen comrades.

Last, we clearly recognize that we are standing on the shoulders of giants in the fields of grief, bereavement, and trauma. We have incorporated their wisdom and knowledge into our book, adapting it to the circumstances of military widowhood.

We have met many extraordinary people while writing this book. Their support and generosity of spirit kept us focused and motivated us through this whole process. We thank them for helping us to make this book as accurate as possible. Any omissions or errors belong to us alone.

Our book would not be complete without a special thank-you to these good folks who, in our opinion, went above and beyond the call of duty: Michael Wardlaw, Director, Casualty Assistance Division, U.S. Navy, for his vision, advocacy, and belief in this book when it was just a good idea; Col. Mary Torgersen, Director, Casualty and Memorial Affairs Operations Center, U.S. Army, who in the midst of an unending op tempo always made time to offer her knowledge and guidance; Rear Adm. Dick Brooks, Commander, Naval Safety Center, U.S. Navy, for his leadership, unwavering support, and motivational good humor; Col. Bob Belkowski (Ret.), for his incredible wealth of knowledge on all facets of the Air Force; Col. Steve Cote, Fleet Marine Officer, Second Fleet, and Col. Bob Fawcett (Ret.), for being good Marines and looking out for the families of all Marines; Brig. Gen. Joe Smith, Commander, U.S. Army Combat Readiness Center, and Maj. Phil Furr (Ret.), two first-rate helo pilots, for providing insight into the mind, heart, and soul of the Army; and last but not least, Elena Serocki, our first editor, for volunteering her insight and organizational skill, which helped us to sharpen our ideas into a clear message and pull our manuscript together.

Our specials thanks to the following:

Diane Atkins
Bruce Baker
Lt. Col. James C. Bates, USA (Ret.)
Lollie Bellski
Maj. Maria Bentinck, USA
Lt. Gen. Martin Berndt, USMC
Chaplain Christian Biscotti, USAF
Lindsay Blanton
Chaplain Dennis Boyle, USCG
Capt. Steve Brasington, MC, USNR
Deb "Murphy" Brown
Capt. John Brown Jr., USN
Col. Penny Burns, USAFR (Ret.)
Col. Walter "Buster" Burns, USAF (Ret.)
Debbie Busch
John Cabeen
Marie Campbell
Lt. Col. Brad Cantrell, USMC
Bonnie Carroll
Maj. Sonya Carter, USA
Paul Clements, PhD, APRN, BC,
    DF-IAFN
Mardy Colling
Chaplain Johnny Cometa, USN
Capt. John D. Cook, USCG (Ret.)
Robert Cullingford
Kenneth J. Doka, PhD
Dee Dora
Lt. Cdr. Lynn Downs, USN
Capt. Bernadette Dozier, USAF
Twila Driver, APRN, BC
Rev. Mr. Bob Durel
Sarah Honaker Dyess
Lt. Cdr. Richard N. East, USCG (Ret.)

Col. Ronnie Ellis, USA
Col. Phil Fain, USAF
Capt. Forrest Faison III, MC, USN
Meg Falk
Mary Fallon
Karen Fisher
Capt. David Forslund, USCG
Capt. Kenneth Franke, USCG (Ret.)
Capt. Dan Franken, USN (Ret.)
Stephanie Frogge
Diane C. Fuller
Chaplain Jack Galle, USN
Vice Adm. Hank Giffin, USN (Ret.)
M.Sgt. Linda Gilbo, USA (Ret.)
Betsy Graham
Rabbi Scott Gurdin
Lee Anne Guzy
Greg Harms
Capt. Paul Heim, USN
Mary Beth Helsel, RN, BSN, CRRN
Karen Hornstein
Cdr. Tom Jarrell, USN (Ret.)
Cdr. Bruce Johnson, USN (Ret.)
Lisa Johnson
Capt. Kenny Jones, USMC
Roger Jorstad
Capt. Tom "TK" Keeley, USN
Gini King
Col. Larry King "Live," USMC
Fred Klinkengerger
Chief Boatswain's Mate
    Eric Kvistad, USCG
Capt. Lou Lalli, USN (Ret.)
Maj. Patrick Lamb, USA

Barbara Lambert, APRN, BC
Marshall "Wardog" Lefavor
Chaplain Karl Lindblad, USN
Brenda Liston
Carla Logan, BS, RN
Lt. Cdr. Jean Lord, NC, USN
Chaplain Bill Maddox, USA (Ret.)
Chaplain John Maurice, USN
Chaplain David McBeth, USN
Jenn McCollum
Capt. Bob Miller, USN (Ret.)
Theresa Miller
Priscilla Mills
Dana Morel
Masako Murphy
Col. J. B. Murray, USAF
Chaplain Andrew Nelko, USN
Machinery Technician
    Chief Alfred P. Orth, USCG
Dave "Hey Joe" Parsons
Edward Perratore
Elena Serocki Perratore
Virginia Perratore
Thomas R. Perry
Chaplain Michael Pumphrey, USN
Lula M. Redmond, MS, RN, LMFT, CT
Darla Reed
Chief Warrant Officer Greg Reese,
    USA (Ret.)
Lt. Col. Wes Rehorn, SF, USA
Senior Chief Boatswain's Mate (SEAL)
    Boyd Renner, USN
Maj. Bill Richards, USA (Ret.)
Rev. Mr. Joe Riss
Anna Roman-Mercado
Elizabeth Rosborg
Daniel Ruiz
Rev. Charles Saglio

Maj. Karl Schelly, USAR
Command Master Chief (AW)
    Paul Schettler, USN
Lt. Col. Arnold A. Schneider, USAF (Ret.)
Maj. Jaime Schofield, USAF
Pam Schroeder, MSN, RN, CHPN
Lt. Col. Ellis Sharadin, USAF (Ret.)
Capt. Jerry K. Shields, CC, USN
Rear Adm. Dennis Sirois, USCG
Col. Walt Slusark, USAR (Ret.)
Sgt. Linda Spruill, Newport News
    Police Department
John Stein
Cdr. Barry J. Stevens, USNR
1st Lt. Alyson Teeter, USAF
Col. Preston Thompson, USAF
Capt. Ruth Torres, USCG
Debbie Turlip
Col. Tom Turlip, USANG
Shari Turner
Chief Warrant Officer
    David E. VanClief, USCG
Lt. Cdr. J. Andrew Van Slyke, MC, USNR
Robert O. Wagner
Lt. Terrence Walsh, USCG
Amy Walton
H. Mark Ward
Mark L. Ward
Michael Wardlaw
Greg Wheless
Chaplain Paul Witt
Mary M. Wong
Rev. Ken Wood
Maj. Stacy Wood, USA (Ret.)
Bill Woodhouse
Lt. Gen. Bruce "Orville" Wright, USAF
Capt. James Yohe, USN
Rabbi Israel Zoberman, DMin

We would also like to thank the Naval Institute Press: Tom Wilkerson, for recognizing the necessity of this book, and all the many fine professionals who helped us through the publication process. A special thank-you to Mary Svikhart for her editorial expertise. Our heartfelt thanks for helping to make this necessary book a reality.

Last, a very personal thank-you from me (Regina) to my husband, Capt. Rich Asaro, USCG (Ret.). His command experience, ongoing dedication to military service, and compassion for those serving our country have enriched our lives together. Certainly, his love and support made writing this book much easier. He is one of our biggest cheerleaders.

ACRONYMS

AFB	air force base
AMTRAC	amphibious armored, tracked personnel carrier
BAH	basic allowance for housing
CACO	Casualty Assistance Calls Officer
CAO	Casualty Assistance Officer
CONUS	continental United States
DEERS	Defense Enrollment Eligibility Reporting System
DIC	Dependency and Indemnity Compensation
DoD	Department of Defense
FLO	Family Liaison Officer
FOIA	Freedom of Information Act
FTC	Federal Trade Commission
HAHO	high altitude, high opening
HMMWV	high mobility, multipurpose wheeled vehicle
ID	identification
IED	improvised explosive device
JAG	Judge Advocate General
MEU	Marine Expeditionary Unit
NCO	noncommissioned officer
PAO	public affairs office
PCS	permanent change of station
PX	post exchange
SAR	search and rescue
SEAL	SEa, Air, and Land
SGLI	Servicemembers' Group Life Insurance
SSN	Social Security number

TDY	temporary duty
URW	un-remarried widow
USDA	United States Department of Agriculture
VA	United States Department of Veterans Affairs
VFR	visual flight rules

MILITARY WIDOW

INTRODUCTION

*W*E WROTE THIS BOOK FOR YOU: the military wife who became a widow. We know you didn't volunteer for widowhood. No wife ever does. But life's tragedies rarely ask for permission.

Your young husband's sudden and untimely death is possibly your first exposure to loss and grief, a difficult way to learn about death. His death most likely propelled you into a tailspin of uncontrollable emotions, thoughts, and actions, the likes of which were new, unfamiliar, and scary. Our experience has taught us that your intense feelings of grief are valid. Many widows feel the same way.

There are many good books available on grief. Some focus on widowhood, and a few target the issues that young widows face. *Military Widow: A Survival Guide* addresses the issues of young widows, but most importantly, speaks to the unique circumstances of military widowhood.

We know firsthand that a military death is fraught with complications not seen in the civilian world. In all likelihood, at the time of your husband's death you were living at a duty station, far away from family and old friends. Your husband's death was probably unexpected, potentially traumatic in nature, possibly in another country, publicized in the media, complicated by his commitment to duty, and compounded by the bureaucracy that follows a military loss. The grief you feel, created by military death, is complex.

Military Widow: A Survival Guide has blended more than ten years of lessons learned from military widows with professional knowledge of grief and traumatic loss. Written in short, easy-to-read chapters, this guide brings together personal profiles of military widows, knowledge of military loss and the issues it generates, guidance from leading grief experts, and the wisdom of military widows who have walked in your shoes.

1

Military Widow: A Survival Guide will:
- provide realistic examples of military loss,
- explain why military grief is complex,
- validate your feelings based on other military widows' experiences,
- echo the deepest feelings of military widows,
- shed light on the unspoken issues of military widowhood,
- deal with the difficult decisions unique to military life,
- support you through sudden, traumatic loss,
- tackle the spiritual quandary often associated with death,
- offer practical advice for dealing with your kids,
- address the changing relationship with your in-laws,
- suggest sensible tips for dating again,
- reveal the dark humor of widows, and
- present insight into personal growth after traumatic loss.

No book will ever cover all that you want to know, and there can never be enough written about your personal loss. We know this from experience.

We also know that military widows struggle to relate to civilian widows they meet in grief groups or other forms of grief support. The circumstances of a military death, and the complex issues it generates, sometimes isolate a military widow, even from other widows. To help you understand that you are not alone, that there *are* other military widows like yourself, we have created fictitious but realistic stories of military loss—and the women who dealt with it—and tied them to the topic of each chapter. These stories illustrate how military widows sort out the specific issues discussed in that chapter. In *Military Widow: A Survival Guide* you will connect with the stories of these widows, identify with the issues facing most military widows, and find a way to work through your grief as a stepping-stone to a new life that awaits you. Life will get better. We want to help you in that journey.

In addition to these stories of other widows, we have included two other features in the chapters.
- The "Lessons Learned" are gathered from the wisdom of those women who have walked the path of military widowhood before you. They are life lessons: learned by trial and error and therefore priceless. Some are profound; others simply reflect the realities of

living through a life-changing loss. We offer them to you because there is no reason for you to reinvent the wheel and figure out these lessons on your own.

- The "Echoes" express the unspoken thoughts and feelings found in the deepest corners of your heart and soul. These echoes turn your often-silent feelings into words and give meaning to the expressions of loss that are now a part of your life. The echoes are the voices of those same military widows who offered you their lessons learned.

This book honors the sacrifices of your husband *and* you, his widow.

PART ONE

Life and Death in the Military

CHAPTER 1

★ ★ ★

THE ULTIMATE SACRIFICE

*t*WO MILITARY MEN GET OUT OF an official government vehicle, checking to make sure they have the correct address. They nervously glance at each other as they gear up to carry out their mission. Each of them dreads the duty he is about to perform. Heads bent, they walk swiftly toward the house.

Inside, a wife watches them walk toward her front door. Noticing the blank expressions on their faces, she thinks, "They look like angels of death." Ice runs through her veins. "They must be lost," she tells herself. In her heart, she knows that something is very, very wrong. She jumps when the doorbell rings and hesitates before answering it, giving herself one final moment of normalcy. She knows when she opens the door, life will never be the same again. With a sense of dread, she lets them in. Once inside her home, the senior officer starts to say, "We regret to inform you. . . ." And, for this wife, time stops.

WIFE MADE WIDOW

Hearing these terrifying words is every military wife's worst nightmare. But, as every wife made widow knows, that life-changing phrase is just the tip of the iceberg, the beginning of the ordeal called military widowhood. More scary moments occur later, long after the funeral and memorial services are over, when it's just you and the remnants of a love and a life you cherished.

This book was written specifically for you, if you have walked in the shoes of this wife and faced the consequences of military widowhood that we describe in the list that follows:

- Your husband died in the military.
- You are too young to be a widow.
- Your world has become a living hell.
- You are scared of your intense feelings of grief.
- You feel like you are going crazy.
- You do not know where you fit in.
- You are lost in the complexities of military grief.

This book is about survival, coping, and growth. It is written with the wisdom of countless military widows. It passes on their personal lessons of victory over grief, and it gives hope as you evolve from wife to widow to woman. You can learn much from those who were widowed before you. Like those brave women, you can also find meaning and joy in the new world into which you were catapulted when your husband died.

An Honorable but Dangerous Job

The Army, Navy, Marine Corps, Air Force, and Coast Guard are made up of hundreds of thousands of men and women of character and integrity. Each has volunteered to protect and defend America and, if need be, make the ultimate sacrifice in its defense. Realistically, every military service member expects to live to a ripe old age. Sometimes, though, life doesn't turn out the way it's planned.

The U.S. military is essential to American safety and security. Since the days of colonial America, bad guys have threatened our freedoms, our values, and our homeland. It is no different today. America's armed forces, and its citizens, have been attacked at home and abroad. We are all affected by this war on terror, but when your husband wears a military uniform, it becomes personal.

★ ★ ★

Lesson Learned
Protecting America is a dangerous profession.

Sometimes They Die

An average of fifteen hundred military servicemen and women die in an active duty status each year (U.S. Department of Defense). Some were killed by hostile fire in faraway places like Somalia, Kuwait, Afghanistan, and Iraq. Others died in terrorist attacks in Lebanon, Saudi Arabia, Yemen, and the United States. A number of our military were killed on training missions. Accidents, both on and off base, claimed some lives, as did disease and illness. A few died by suicide or murder. No matter how these military men and women died, one thing is certain: they were the best of the best— all strong, intelligent, committed, and patriotic. And they died young.

FREEDOM'S PRICE

Our country pays tribute to its fallen service members with time-honored traditions and public displays of remembrance. We bury them with military honors and build memorials to their sacrifice. We recall their professionalism and their commitment to duty, honor, and country. Every one of these men and women, however, had a name, a face, a personality, and a family who loved them. The widow left behind has lost much more than a heroic service member; her loss is life changing. From this point forward, time will be measured by the years spent with her husband and the years spent without him.

★ ★ ★

Echo

*"Protecting America does have a price,
and for me it was my husband's life."*

WIDOWS LIKE YOU

Throughout this book, you'll read dozens of realistic stories about widows and the men they loved, men who died while serving our country. A few of the widows are not old enough to legally buy a drink. Others were making plans for their life when their husbands retired from active duty. A number of women were pregnant or already had children when their husbands died; some were cheated out of motherhood. They came from all over the United States, and even its territories. The widows you'll read about are of many races, religions, and nationalities. Their husbands served in every service branch, as officers or enlisted personnel of every rank and rate. As usually happens in the military, most of these men died suddenly and violently. All too often, their remains were unviewable, and occasionally no remains were recovered to bury.

In this chapter and the next one, we will personally introduce you to five widows, one from each branch of our armed forces. You will see that these women are a lot like you: typical military wives, until their worst fear became reality.

In our first story, a Marine widow is left with an infant son when her husband is killed in Iraq.

KC and Courtney

KC, Courtney, and their infant son, Josh, were the all-American family. Originally from South Bend, Indiana, they came from simple, hardworking families who were surprised, but supportive, when KC joined the Marine Corps after his college graduation. KC was profoundly affected by the September 11 attacks and felt that joining the Marines was a way for him to do something for his country.

Courtney didn't know much about military life, but if that's what KC wanted, then that's what she wanted. They made many adjustments in the first two years of their marriage, including adapting to military life and the surprise arrival of their son. Life on the base in Southern California was good, and Courtney liked being a wife and mother.

When KC's battalion got orders to Iraq, Courtney was worried. KC explained that he and his Marines were well trained and well equipped. He was confident they could handle anything that might be thrown at them. On the day he left, KC asked Courtney to be strong, take good care of Josh, and start planning for his homecoming. He'd be back before she knew it.

KC had been in Iraq about six months. Initially, his battalion took daily casualties, but the last few weeks had been good ones, and the casualty rate was light. As a first lieutenant and an infantry platoon commander, KC saw some fierce fighting, and some of his men had been killed or seriously wounded.

One fateful day, KC's platoon was tasked to clear a warehouse complex of insurgent fighters in Ramadi. While shouting instructions to his first squad leader, KC was shot in the head by a sniper. He died instantly. Halfway around the world, Courtney became a widow at twenty-four.

On the day KC was killed, Courtney recalled that Josh woke up screaming. Nothing she said or did would comfort him. That was the first time Courtney had ever seen Josh scream like that, and she was afraid something was seriously wrong with her baby. Now looking back, Courtney realized that Josh's screaming fit happened on the day KC was killed. She wonders if, in his own eight-month-old way, Josh knew he would never see his father alive again.

In our next story, a young Navy widow, desperately in love with her new husband, had a hard time believing he was killed in a shipboard accident.

Jaime and Selina

Twenty-three-year-old Jaime was proud to be in the Navy. He had grown up watching his parents struggle to make a new life for themselves and their children in Hartford, Connecticut, after they immigrated to the United States. As a boy, Jaime sometimes felt like a foreigner, even though he was the first in his family to be born in America. That was because he spoke English with an accent. In his neighborhood, everyone was Hispanic.

In the Navy, though, Jaime found a new identity. He was an American Sailor, stationed aboard a guided missile cruiser that was homeported in San Diego. Jaime quickly became qualified in several watch-station positions on the ship.

While stationed in San Diego, Jaime met Selina. He thought she was the most beautiful woman in the world. After a proper period of dating and getting to know one another, Jaime asked Selina's father for permission to marry his daughter. With her father's blessing, Selina and Jaime were married in a mission church in Old Town.

Selina loved Jaime as much as he loved her. She didn't understand too much about the Navy, though. Sometimes at night, she would worry about how she would live through six months without Jaime while his ship was deployed. Even in a pre-deployment mode, the ship was always going out to sea for a few days on workups.

Late one Tuesday afternoon, Selina, who had just gotten home from work and was taking a nap, was awakened by the doorbell. She was surprised to find three grim-faced individuals in white Navy uniforms at her door. Selina could not understand why they were there, because Jaime was at sea. There was a chaplain, a chief who spoke Spanish, and a woman who said she was a CACO. They told her there had been a serious accident at sea on board the cruiser and that Jaime was involved in it.

These Navy officials explained that Jaime, a machinist's mate second class, had just taken the watch in the ship's engine room when a fuel oil hose ruptured. The engine room was engulfed in fire and thick, black smoke. Jaime was incapacitated and unable to get out.

When he was rescued, Jaime was unconscious, with severe burns over ninety percent of his body. He was given emergency treatment by the ship's corpsman and evacuated by helicopter to Balboa Naval Medical Center. Jaime never regained consciousness and was pronounced dead at the hospital.

Because of his burns, Selina did not see Jaime's body. She had a hard time believing he was dead. He was so young, and they had so many plans for their future. Selina kept hoping the Navy had made a mistake. She just knew in her heart that when the ship returned to port the following week, Jaime would be on it.

In the next chapter, we will introduce you to the widow of an Army NCO (noncommissioned officer) who was killed in the Pentagon on September 11, an Air Force pilot's widow, and the widow of a warrant officer in the Coast Guard.

PUTTING IT ALL TOGETHER

Throughout the history of our country, those who chose military service believed it was a higher calling. Some gave all in our country's service. The rendering of honors to these fallen servicemen and women has been a long, respectful, and enduring tradition. But the unsung heroes of these losses are the widows and their families who must face the future without their Soldier, Sailor, Marine, Airman, or Coast Guardsman.

CHAPTER 2

★ ★ ★

WHO IS THE MILITARY WIDOW?

*Y*OU ARE A SLICE OF THE CULTURE OF AMERICA, a smorgasbord of ages, races, nationalities, and backgrounds. You are all individual and unique women, united by the bond that you married a service member who died while serving his country.

On your wedding day, you probably didn't realize that, in addition to marrying your husband, you married into the lifestyle and culture of his service branch. You weren't just a wife but a military wife, and as the saying goes, "It's the toughest job in the military." This is true no matter what branch your husband served in.

As you have learned, the military is a world unto itself, and—while you may have lived, worked, and raised your children in a civilian community—something about you was different. As a military wife or widow, you

- moved every one to four years, sometimes overseas,
- have close friends stationed all over the world,
- carry a military ID card,
- recite your husband's SSN (Social Security number) as easily as your own,
- use military medicine,
- may have lived in base housing,
- may have been active in spouses clubs,
- came to accept that the military is more than a job,
- can handle emergencies on your own (or know whom to call),

- sometimes sent your husband off for six to twelve months at a time, and
- speak the language of acronyms of the Army, Navy, Marine Corps, Air Force, or Coast Guard.

Some women truly enjoyed military life. Others did not and struggled with it almost on a daily basis. No matter how you felt about life in the military, it took a great deal of dedication and sacrifice on your part.

It takes a special woman to handle military life. Having been military wives ourselves, we believe a successful military wife develops the necessary life skills and attributes. To succeed, she is:

- independent—she thinks for herself and her family;
- matriarchal—she holds the family together;
- flexible—she adjusts to changing circumstances;
- a problem solver—she looks for solutions, not roadblocks;
- resilient—she presses on no matter what the obstacle;
- tenacious—she fights for what she believes is right; and
- supportive—she accepts that she cannot always come first.

Whether you were a military wife for six months or twenty years, the nature of military life forced you to develop these life skills better and faster than women your age who are not connected to the armed forces. You also have other coping skills, learned from dealing with situations in your family or on the job. All of these combined skills, plus an inner strength that you aren't aware of yet, will help you to survive in the days, weeks, months, and years ahead as a military widow.

★ ★ ★

Lesson Learned
The life skills you developed as a military wife will help you cope with military widowhood.

It seems like only yesterday you were a wife, coping with the normal issues of military life. But then the unexpected happened, and a new label and identity were forced upon you. Even as a military widow, you still don't fit into a particular mold. So, who are you?

- You are any age, but definitely young. You may be a newlywed or a woman with kids in high school. Most likely, you have a few dependent children at home.

- You have a high school diploma or a GED. Maybe you are a college graduate with an advanced degree.
- You are a stay-at-home mom and were a single parent when your husband deployed.
- You have a part-time job outside of your home. Or, you have your own career in the military or civilian world.
- You are Caucasian, African-American, Asian, Hispanic, Native American, or some combination of races and cultures.
- You are tall, short, plump, skinny, or any size in between.
- You are from central California, a small town in Missouri, a suburb of Atlanta, an exit off the New Jersey turnpike, or almost anywhere in the world.
- You are Christian, Jewish, Muslim, Hindu, Buddhist, or have beliefs all your own.
- You are living away from home at a duty station, perhaps on another continent.
- Your husband drove a Humvee, flew airplanes, fixed engines, launched missiles, repaired computers, cooked meals, inspected seagoing vessels, or carried a rifle.

★ ★ ★

Lesson Learned

Military widows come in all ages, races, nationalities, and religions, regardless of your husband's rate, rank, or service branch.

Yesterday, you worried about money, kids, and getting rid of those pesky pounds from your last pregnancy. Then your world turned inside out and upside down. Without warning, your life changed forever.

In the stories in the last chapter, you met an officer's wife and an enlisted wife, very different women, who shared the same fate of military widowhood when their husbands died suddenly and far away from home. In our next story, you will meet an Army widow who was looking forward to life after the military. But then her world was changed forever one September morning.

Darrell and Savannah

Darrell and Savannah met in basic training at Fort Jackson, South Carolina, when they were just kids. Nineteen years later, they were in their late thirties, and Darrell was talking about retiring. Their two children were in high school and, in a few short years, it would be just the two of them again. They were looking forward to this new chapter in their lives. In his last tour, Darrell was working in the Army G1 at the Pentagon. Savannah, who was a civil servant and an Army Reservist, was working in the U.S. Army Materiel Command at nearby Fort Belvoir.

On a particularly beautiful September day in the Washington, D.C., area, Darrell arrived at the Pentagon in a good mood. Feeling especially upbeat, he called Savannah at her office, wanting to take her out to dinner that evening. That was the last conversation Darrell and Savannah would have. The date was September 11, 2001.

Savannah was shocked when she heard of the initial attacks on the World Trade Center. But when the Pentagon was hit, she became fearful for Darrell's safety. She rationalized, however, that the Pentagon was a massive complex. The odds were in her favor that Darrell was okay. She needed to remain calm and optimistic.

Savannah was also worried about her children, who were at school in nearby Alexandria. With cell phone service jammed, there was no way to contact either Darrell or her kids. Savannah wouldn't rest easy until she had spoken with all of them. Later that evening, with the kids safely at home, Savannah still hadn't heard from Darrell. Her fear for his safety increased. She held out hope for the man she loved, despite the churning anxiety that was building up within her.

Because of the mass confusion in the D.C. area, Savannah did not find out until the next morning that her husband was killed in the Pentagon attack. Darrell, a senior personnel NCO, was stationed in the part of the Pentagon that was destroyed in the terrorist attacks on America. He was posthumously awarded a Purple Heart.

Now Savannah has trouble dealing with beautiful, sunny days, because they remind her of the morning of September 11.

In our next story, an Air Force widow must come to terms with the fact that her husband crashed at sea and no remains were recovered.

Jack and Cindy

Jack was a pilot in the Air Force and the Operations Group commander at Langley AFB (Air Force Base). Jack was well liked and respected by both his subordinates and his superiors. He was married to Cindy, ten years younger, who was as well liked as her husband.

Jack was one of those pilots who was born to fly. He was a seasoned pilot, with more than twenty-eight hundred hours in the cockpit of various fighter aircraft. Jack saw combat during the first Gulf War and earned three air medals.

One ordinary Thursday evening in August, Jack was flying a two-ship, night intercept mission in an F-15C, approximately a hundred miles off the coast of Virginia. Without warning, the aircraft disappeared from the radar screen. The accident investigation board concluded the cause of the crash was probably spatial disorientation. All indications were that Jack did not bail out of the aircraft but most likely rode it into the water. Search crews didn't find, much less recover, the aircraft wreckage or Jack's body.

Cindy couldn't believe the news when the notification team came to their house. After all, Jack had flown combat missions over Iraq and Kuwait. There was no possible way he could have died somewhere out over the Atlantic Ocean on a routine training flight. He was too good a pilot to let that happen.

At the wing memorial service, Cindy was presented with a folded American flag and a shadow box of Jack's medals, ribbons, and rank insignia, which highlighted his career. While she was grateful for the tribute to Jack, all Cindy could think was, "Please end this nightmare and give me my husband back."

In the last of our five stories, a Coast Guard widow wrestles with her anger after her husband's preventable death.

Charlie and Cameron

Charlie, thirty-five, was a warrant officer in the Coast Guard.

He was stationed in New Orleans, where he worked as a marine safety inspector. He and Cameron, a year younger than Charlie, had been married fourteen years and had three children. For the most part, Charlie and Cameron loved the opportunity to live in different parts of the country. New Orleans was a good duty station. Cameron frequently planned weekend trips to explore the history and cuisine of southern Louisiana.

Cameron liked that Charlie was in marine safety. Although he worked long hours and traveled occasionally, he was home most of the time.

Late one May, Charlie and several other Coast Guard inspectors were assigned to perform a routine inspection on a 190-foot oil barge in dry dock for its biennial certificate of inspection. The inspection included a physical examination of each cargo tank for corrosion and leaks. Before the inspection crew could go into the tank, a gas-free chemist had to certify the tank as "Safe for Men and Safe for Fire."

Charlie was certain this inspection had been done but that the certificate just hadn't been posted yet. So, when he walked past one of the tanks and saw a yard worker lying at the foot of the ladder, he assumed the man had had a heart attack. Charlie immediately went down to assist him. Thirty seconds after reaching the bottom of the ladder, Charlie passed out from a lack of oxygen. He was dead three minutes later. Another Coast Guard inspector who went looking for Charlie found both men.

The accident report stated that Charlie had died of asphyxiation. Cameron couldn't understand or accept how this accident happened. She viewed both deaths as senseless and preventable.

PUTTING IT ALL TOGETHER

What you learn from these five stories is that death in the military does not discriminate by service branch, rate, rank, race, culture, or nationality. While each of the servicemen died differently, a common bond unites the women we described here, the bond of being a military widow. It does not matter what uniform your husband wore or what rank he achieved. All military widows walk the same path, one filled with unknown and sometimes scary obstacles, as they work to survive their loss and cope with the feelings, thoughts, and issues that confront them.

In the next chapter, and all that follow it, we will share more stories of military widows and the issues and challenges they face in their journey through military loss and grief, and how they responded to those challenges.

PART TWO

Military Grief Is Complex

CHAPTER 3

★ ★ ★

YOUR LIFE EXPERIENCES

Jake and Ashley

Ashley could not remember a time in her life when she didn't know Jake. The two had grown up in Laramie, Wyoming, and Jake was always in her life: first as a skinny little kid with a skateboard, then as an annoying tease in middle school, and later as a boyfriend in high school. Ashley's and Jake's parents reluctantly gave their blessing to the marriage when Ashley discovered she was pregnant in her senior year of high school. Now twenty years old and living on post at Fort Riley, Kansas, she was the mother of a two-year-old son and three months pregnant with their second child—another boy, according to the doctor.

Ashley was at the commissary when the Casualty Notification Officer came knocking at her door. She returned home with a car full of groceries and a cranky toddler to find an official Army vehicle in front of her house. Ashley learned that her Jake, a corporal serving in Afghanistan, had been killed in a firefight.

The following days and weeks were a blur for Ashley. Both sets of families wanted her to move back to Wyoming immediately, which she did just after the memorial service on post for Jake and the other Soldier killed with him.

It was especially painful for both families when they learned that Jake was killed by friendly fire. "I can't accept how my son died," Jake's grief-stricken father cried.

As the primary next of kin, Ashley was entitled to a Fatal Accident Family Briefing by the Army about the circumstances of

Jake's death. Because both families were close, Ashley asked his parents, as well as her own, to be present at the briefing. It was incredibly tough on the families to hear of Jake's last moments. Knowing the details helped them, though—they had imagined a far worse scenario of actions and events.

*M*ILITARY GRIEF IS COMPLEX for a number of reasons. Let's start by looking at you, personally, and your life in general at the time your husband died. These factors can greatly influence how you react and cope with his death. We will focus on five aspects of your life: your age, your previous experience with death, children, your duty station, and deployments.

YOUR AGE

In our American culture, we usually think of a widow as an older, matronly lady. We do not picture a young woman in jeans trying to balance a baby on her hip. In reality, most military widows are in their twenties, thirties, or forties.

Prior to being widowed, you had other things on your mind, such as being married and raising children. Your life was busy and full, and your future was filled with hopes and dreams for yourself, your husband, and your family.

Widowhood was not a part of your thoughts and, we hope, not a part of your immediate world. You knew that deaths sometimes occurred in the military, but somewhere in the back of your mind you thought, "It can't happen in my husband's unit." Or, God forbid, if it should happen in his command, you hoped and prayed, "It won't happen to him."

Whether in the civilian or military world, being widowed when you're young isn't a normal event. It is viewed as abnormal, atypical, odd, and unusual, by both the widow and the people who encounter her. When an older woman says she's widowed, the normal response is, "I'm sorry." When a young woman says she's widowed, the response goes something like this: "Oh—I'm so sorry! What happened?"

In our post–September 11 world, the reaction to military loss is more intense and sympathetic, but young widowhood, especially military widowhood, seems to need an explanation.

As a young widow you may feel like a sideshow in the circus. People sometimes regard you as a curious oddity. Because you aren't supposed to be a widow at such a young age, you don't fit in anywhere. The world tells you that you're not married, but you don't feel single, not in the same way your never-married or divorced friends are single. You are probably not comfortable in either the married or the single world. You may wonder where you fit in now, especially if you don't know any other young widows. You likely feel alone and maybe isolated.

★   ★   ★

Lesson Learned

Young widowhood always *requires an explanation.*

YOUR PREVIOUS EXPERIENCE WITH DEATH

The death of your husband is an intense and intensely personal loss, more so than the deaths of grandparents, parents, or siblings. Even if you have lost a family member or a close friend, nothing could have prepared you for the sudden and possibly traumatic death of your husband. Your relationship as husband and wife was a personal and intimate one; you had a physical, emotional, spiritual, social, and legal attachment to each other.

The death of a spouse ranks number one on the list of stressful life events (Holmes and Rahe, 1967). Because you are young, your husband's untimely death may be your first real encounter with death, making it seem surreal.

★   ★   ★

Lesson Learned

You are never prepared for the death of a young husband.

CHILDREN

The whole question of children makes young widowhood harder. If your husband deployed regularly, you were probably the backbone of the family. You were the one the kids saw as the ever-present parent and primary caregiver. And, you still are. When your military husband dies, your kids, no matter what their ages, need you more than ever to be strong and maintain some sense of normalcy in their lives, even though the rest of your world is in ruins. Being strong for your kids, however, probably does not leave you much time or energy to take care of yourself or grieve for your husband.

Many military widows are young, and a number of them are pregnant or have newborns when their husbands die. If this describes you, then you know the cauldron of emotions that erupts when new motherhood collides with widowhood. Many women feel they are robbed of the joy of motherhood. Some believe the hormonal roller coaster of pregnancy, childbirth, and widowhood makes them feel out of sorts and often out of control. Still others agree that caring for a brand-new baby leaves them too exhausted to focus on their own physical and emotional needs.

Not having children can likewise complicate grieving for your husband. Maybe you and your husband had postponed starting a family or were trying to get pregnant when he was killed. With his death, your hope of bearing his children is gone. This is another loss for you to confront and grieve. You may have other children in your life, but you will never have *his* children.

★ ★ ★

Lesson Learned
Children, whether you have them or not,
complicate young widowhood.

Your Duty Station

There is a good chance you were living far from home when your husband died. Because you are young, you probably haven't been living away from your family for any length of time. Your roots and a good many of your emotional connections may still be centered in the place where you grew up. There is the old saying, "Home is where the military sends us," and that is true, to an extent. Home is wherever you are stationed, but when tragedy strikes, we like to surround ourselves with family and old friends, people with whom we share history and feel comfortable, safe, and secure.

In addition to your assigned casualty officer, your husband's unit probably came to your aid and assistance. Members of his unit and their spouses, whom you may have regarded as your military family, usually help to take care of the essential human needs: cooking meals, caring for the kids, answering the phone and e-mail, and helping your stunned relatives with transportation and motels. Their support is real and genuine, but as you know, at some point after the funeral or memorial service, they go back to their own lives. This is one of the first occurrences of distancing and separation from the military you will face in the coming days and weeks.

★ ★ ★
Lesson Learned
*When you were first told of your husband's death, the people
you relied on were not likely to be family or longtime friends.*

DEPLOYMENTS

If your husband deployed regularly, you were probably accustomed to having him away from home for weeks or months at a time. If he was killed while he was deployed, the reality of his death was harder for you to accept. Even after his remains were returned to the United States and the funeral and memorial services were over, you may have found yourself thinking—and believing—that your husband would be coming home when his unit returned to post. The truth is that the reality of your husband's death comes in small slices. You will face another harsh slice of reality when your husband's unit comes home without him.

★ ★ ★
Lesson Learned
*If your husband was killed on deployment, you expected him
to come home when his command returned.*

PUTTING IT ALL TOGETHER

Some of the factors that make military grief complex—such as your age, your previous experience with death, and the whole question of children—also make grief harder for the young widow in the civilian world. But when you add deployments and duty stations on top of a young age, dependent children, and little experience with death, your grief can be decidedly more complicated.

CHAPTER 4

★ ★ ★

YOUR HUSBAND'S LIFE AND DEATH

Luther and Tanya

Luther was one fine Marine. Ramrod straight and fit and trim, the master sergeant belonged on a recruiting poster. Not only did he look like a Marine, but he also lived his life in a way that reflected the very ethos of the Marine Corps. Out in the field or back in garrison, he was professional, dedicated, and above reproach. Any Marine who knew him—his superiors, peers, or subordinates—respected him as a man and as a Marine. At thirty-five, Luther had seventeen years in, and he planned to stay until the Marine Corps told him to go home.

Luther was as respected out of uniform as he was in uniform. He sang in the church choir, and when he was not deployed, he helped coach his son's Little League team. He also had a passion for cooking and claimed he made the best barbequed ribs east of the Mississippi.

Luther gave Tanya and the Corps credit for making a man out of him. Married just over fifteen years, Tanya saw a side of Luther that was reserved only for her. Her tough Marine husband was like putty in her hands, a fact that was known, but unspoken, between them.

The master sergeant was in Iraq ten months when he was killed. While checking in with his Marines who were manning a checkpoint in Baqubah, a suicide bomber rode up to the checkpoint and blew himself up. Luther was one of five Marines killed by the force of the explosion, which created a crater twenty feet wide and four feet deep. Because Luther was closest to the bomber, he took the full brunt of the blast. Only partial remains could be recovered and sent home to Tanya and her sons.

*Y*OU HAVE ALREADY SEEN HOW MILITARY GRIEF is complicated by unique circumstances in your life. In this chapter, we will look at your husband. We will help you grasp the very core of his life and death, and how it affects you as a military widow. We will talk about the significance of your husband's age, your relationship with him, his values and sense of purpose, and the circumstances of his death.

YOUR HUSBAND'S AGE

No matter how old your husband was, one thing is certain: he died too young. When you and your spouse are about the same age, death jolts your sense of security and stability. Your own sense of immortality is threatened, too. You are confronted with the fact that neither you nor your husband is invincible, or immune to danger and death.

Before your husband died, life may have been chaotic at times, but for the most part, it was predictable, even if predictability meant regular PCS (permanent change of station) moves halfway around the world. Your life probably followed the traditional pattern of growing up, getting married, and raising a family. Now, with your husband's early death, your guarantee of normalcy and predictability has been shattered, and you don't know what to expect next. You may feel vulnerable, exposed, and defenseless. All the rules of life changed, and you can't trust the world anymore. Death is no longer something that happens in the future, when you get older. It barged into your life without asking, took a seat at your kitchen table, and cannot be kicked out the back door.

★ ★ ★

Lesson Learned

Death erased predictability, safety, and security from your life.

YOUR RELATIONSHIP WITH YOUR HUSBAND

Like many military widows, you may have been married just a short time when your husband died. This is especially hard, and you may feel cheated, because neither you nor your husband ended your marriage willingly. Grief experts Reed and Greenwald (1991) say the greater the bonds of attachment and love between a husband and wife, the greater the pain of separation and loss will be for the surviving spouse.

Let's say your husband was the love of your life, your soul mate, your best friend, and your source of strength in times of crisis. The death of this important person, and the loss of your relationship with him, deepens your grief and magnifies the intensity of your pain. What you long for—the comfort and safety of being with him—has been stolen from you now and for the rest of your earthly days.

Gone are the promise and hope of a full life together, and the dreams you shared in each other's arms in the middle of the night. Gone are the plans you made for your lives: a family, the home you wanted to own one day, the careers you planned, the duty stations you hoped for, and the chance to celebrate your children's birthdays, graduations, and weddings. Gone are the companionship and love you thought would last a lifetime.

★ ★ ★

Echo
"I have precious few memories, but a lifetime of
unfulfilled dreams."

If your husband died later in his career, you lost the opportunity to spend time together once the children grew up and left home, to become reacquainted with one another as you enter the next phase of your life. Gone, too, are the dreams and plans for the retirement toward which you both worked for many years.

Even if your husband was not the great love of your life, and there were more lows than highs in your marriage, death permanently ended your relationship with him. It denied the two of you the opportunity to improve your marriage and make it work.

YOUR HUSBAND'S VALUES AND SENSE OF PURPOSE

In our country, military service is once again viewed with pride and respect. Since September 11, 2001, the need to protect and defend our country has intensified because the danger to America and its citizens is real. Although it is not often discussed casually or lightly, military men often have deep-seated feelings of patriotism, moral purpose, and personal responsibility.

Your husband chose to be part of the military, and this speaks volumes about his character and integrity. He wore his uniform with pride. You may not have fully understood the significance of your husband's service, but his commitment to duty, honor, and country set him apart and made him different. He likely believed his military service was more than just a job. Most military men feel it's the right thing to do for themselves, their families, and their country.

It is exceptionally hard to accept the death of someone you see as having a purpose to his life, and this acceptance is further complicated when that person dies young. This is especially true in the case of military service members, who often die young and for a cause. All who serve in our armed forces give something of themselves. Your husband gave it all. The world is cheated by the loss of men like your husband.

★ ★ ★

Lesson Learned
*Who your husband was, and what he stood for,
make your loss harder to accept.*

THE CIRCUMSTANCES OF YOUR HUSBAND'S DEATH

There is no easy way to lose a husband. While some servicemen die or are killed in the same manner as civilians, many also die in ways that are unique to the military. Each type of death is fraught with particular circumstances that affect how you cope with your husband's death. We can divide military deaths into two general categories: hostile action and non–hostile action.

HOSTILE-ACTION DEATHS

If your husband was killed by hostile action, there is a good chance his death was violent and there was trauma to his body. It may have been badly damaged, or, perhaps, only partial remains were recovered. In rare occasions where multiple deaths occurred under horrific conditions, such as the destruction of the World Trade Center on September 11, the remains of many victims were commingled and could not be separated.

With many hostile-action deaths, the body is not viewable. You may find it impossible to believe your husband is dead if you can't see, touch, or hold his body. In these circumstances, a small part of you will likely cling to the hope of his returning one day.

★ ★ ★

Echo

"I imagined some terrible mistake had been made—
the Army placed the wrong body inside that closed casket;
my husband had amnesia and was in a foreign hospital;
he was picked up in the middle of the ocean by a foreign freighter;
or he washed ashore on a remote island."

The very nature of wartime deaths can also make it difficult for you to get specific information about your husband's death. If he was killed in action, for instance, the details surrounding his death, final actions, or last words may be sketchy at best or simply unknown. These details may also be withheld from you because of an investigation or the classified nature of his mission. These situations can create quite an emotional or psychological problem. When you don't know the facts about your husband's death, you imagine all sorts of horrors he might have endured in his last moments.

There are other situations where, for example, your husband was killed in the middle of a battle, but the fighting showed no signs of stopping. This could make it impossible for his comrades to retrieve his body immediately. Once his body has been recovered, it can take days or weeks for the military to properly identify it, prepare his remains for burial or cremation, and release them to you.

NON–HOSTILE–ACTION DEATHS

In addition to hostile-action deaths, there is an average of fifteen hundred non-hostile-action deaths each year. These deaths include training accidents in the line of duty, on- and off-base accidents, homicides, suicides, and illnesses.

Like hostile-action deaths, training accidents in the line of duty are sudden, random, and preventable, and they usually cause damage or mutilation to the body. Similar to wartime deaths, training deaths are messy, and it can take a long time to recover and identify remains. Because training accidents require an investigation, information about your husband's death can be sparse or delayed for months or years, denying you a timely explanation of how and why he died.

Other kinds of nonhostile deaths include accidents, homicides, suicides, and illnesses. Accidents can occur on- or off-base, or they can be recreational in nature. Car, truck, and motorcycle accidents are common causes of nonhostile deaths in the military. Any type of accidental death is sudden and devastating, no matter how it happens.

Just like in the civilian community, homicides and suicides occur more than you realize. Like other sudden deaths, they leave the surviving spouse with a great deal of anguish and torment, as well as other difficult issues that are specific to the nature of those deaths.

Your husband may have died suddenly from a medical cause, such as heart attack or stroke, while he was on active duty. Or, he may have been diagnosed with a terminal illness and, as a result, was medically retired. Regardless of the cause, and sometimes without clear and noticeable warning signs, this type of death is unexpected.

★ ★ ★
Lesson Learned
Most military deaths are sudden and random;
they often cause trauma to the body that leaves the remains
unsuitable—or unavailable—for viewing.

PUTTING IT ALL TOGETHER

In this chapter, we explored many aspects relating to your husband: who he was, how he chose to live his life, your relationship with him, and how he died. While people in the military die in some of the same ways as civilians, many also die in ways unique to the military. These facets of your husband's life and death, combined with your life experiences and the culture of the military, contribute to the complexity of the grief you feel.

CHAPTER 5

★ ★ ★

THE UNIQUE CULTURE
OF THE MILITARY

Todd and Jenn

Todd and Jenn were dual-career Navy. They met at the U.S. Naval Academy and were married in the chapel there in the whirlwind week after graduation and commissioning. Todd spent much of the first year of their marriage alone at Naval Air Station Pensacola, going through flight school, while his wife, a Supply Corps officer, was stationed at the Fleet Industrial Supply Center in Norfolk, Virginia.

The separation had its rewards, however, as he earned his "Wings of Gold" and was assigned to the fleet replacement squadron of F/A-18 Hornets, based at Oceana in nearby Virginia Beach. Todd and Jenn were finally stationed together, and he was flying fighters. Life was better than good.

One day in mid-January, the squadron was conducting carrier qualifications on an aircraft carrier steaming sixty miles off the Virginia coast. While Todd was attempting to land his aircraft on the flight deck, the arresting cable snapped, and his aircraft bounced off the flight deck and fell into the sea. The carrier's SAR (search and rescue) helicopter was immediately on scene, but Todd had no opportunity to eject. He was trapped in the cockpit as his plane sank. Struggling to release his harness and escape, Todd's last thought was of Jenn, who went from newlywed to widow in less than thirty seconds.

Jenn buried Todd at Arlington National Cemetery with full military honors. As the rituals of the military funeral brought others to tears, Jenn stood stoically beside her young husband's casket, a faraway look in her green eyes. Some commented she was holding up rather well. Little did they know that Jenn was physically exhausted, emotionally numb, and psychologically fragile.

The squadron memorial service for Todd was held the following week at the base chapel. At the end of the service, a Missing Man formation of Hornets screeched overhead in a final tribute to Todd. A lone aircraft accelerated and climbed away from the formation, disappearing too quickly into the low cloud cover. Watching the solitary Hornet, Jenn nodded and thought, "Todd would like that."

A number of Todd's classmates from the academy and flight school came to the memorial service and, after the flyby, they went to the officers club for the reception. Not knowing how to deal with Todd's death, they toasted his memory and told "Todd stories." For Jenn, this was like old times, and for just a few moments, she felt like Todd was alive again.

*i*T IS A LIVING NIGHTMARE when your husband dies suddenly and you are left a young widow and possibly a single mother. This loss is further complicated when you surround it with the unique culture of the military. As you are well aware, the military has a rule or regulation for everything, and death is no exception.

In this chapter, we will help you understand how the military culture influences you and your grief, both in the immediate days and weeks after your husband's death, and on an ongoing basis. We will explore some of the major ways in which a loss in the military is different from a death in the civilian world.

These immediate differences include: the notification process; the role of the casualty officer; the military funeral; the memorial service; the public nature of a military death; military cemeteries; and autopsy and investigation reports. The presence of ongoing reminders—such as national holidays, military connections, and continuing ties to the military system—further complicate military loss.

IMMEDIATE DIFFERENCES

THE NOTIFICATION PROCESS

Because of television news coverage, e-mail, and cell phones, you may have heard of a death or deaths in your husband's unit even before the command was ready to make notifications. Perhaps all you heard through the command grapevine was that someone was killed. You may have spent anxious, gut-wrenching time trying to figure out who was safe—and who was not.

★ ★ ★

Echo

"When the military comes to visit in Class A uniforms
in the middle of the afternoon,
you know your husband isn't coming home ever again."

Movies and television have brought into our homes the image of a somber military officer notifying the next of kin about a young serviceman's death. Hollywood gets it right—most of the time. But no matter how many times you have watched this scene played out, you can't believe it's happening to you when you see the official government vehicle outside your house and military men or women walking up to your door. You know they are bringing bad news.

The process of notification is similar in each of the service branches, and the military tries its best to tell you this devastating news carefully and respectfully. There is no easy way, however, to tell a young wife that her husband is dead, just as there is no easy way to hear it.

★ ★ ★

Lesson Learned

There is no easy way to find out your husband is dead.

THE ROLE OF THE CASUALTY OFFICER

You were assigned a casualty officer even before you knew you were a widow. In the Army, they are CAOs (Casualty Assistance Officers); in the Air Force, they are FLOs (Family Liaison Officers); and in the Navy, Marine Corps, and Coast Guard, they are CACOs (Casualty Assistance Calls Officers).

In the Army and Air Force, a separate individual notifies you of your husband's death (in the Army the title is "Casualty Notification Officer"), and then your CAO or FLO works with you after the official notification. In the Navy and Marine Corps, notification is a part of your CACO's responsibility.

The duties and responsibilities of the casualty officer are sometimes misunderstood by the military widow and her family—and occasionally by the casualty officers themselves.

Regardless of your husband's service branch, the casualty officer's duties are generally the same. His or her job is to be your primary point of contact with the military in the days, weeks, and months after your husband's death. Initially, your casualty officer will help to meet your immediate needs, given your family, financial, or domestic circumstances. He or she will work to ensure that your husband's remains are returned to you as quickly as possible and to assist you in making funeral, memorial, or interment arrangements. Your casualty officer will process the benefits to which you and your family are entitled and assist you with FOIA (Freedom of Information Act) requests for accident investigations and autopsy reports. He or she will guide you through the avalanche of paperwork that is a part of any death, either military or civilian.

Your casualty officer is not a trained grief therapist or psychologist; he or she is simply a military service member, much like your husband. Casualty assistance is usually collateral duty, and it is not easy for three important reasons:

- your husband's death is a blunt reminder that men and women die in the military;
- it is personally painful to witness the profound sorrow of the families left behind; and
- as every military widow knows, there is very little anyone can say or do that will make her feel better.

Some casualty officers are very good at this difficult duty. Others struggle with it and sometimes end up inflicting additional emotional distress upon the widow. Most casualty officers try to do a professional, sensitive, and caring job, understanding that they are helping the widow of a fallen service member.

Working with your casualty officer is usually an emotionally charged experience. The casualty officer is often a complete stranger, yet you must trust him or her to assist you in making major decisions at the worst time of your life. When their casualty responsibility to you is finished, they will return to their normal duty. After spending so much time with this person in an intensely personal situation, it is often another sudden loss when he or she is not there on a regular basis.

★　★　★
Lesson Learned
Death does not bring out the best in anyone, and
that is true of widows—and casualty officers.

THE MILITARY FUNERAL

A military funeral is a time-honored ceremony, full of ritual and tradition. Even more so than the notification process, a military funeral is recognized, revered, and respected for all that it is and all that it stands for. It stirs up an assortment of powerful emotions within us, many of which mere words cannot describe.

From privates to presidents, all military funerals are basically the same: the flag-draped coffin, the echo of a rifle salute, the haunting melody of "Taps," and an American flag folded in a neat triangle of white stars on a sea of blue cradled in a widow's arms. With these rituals and symbols, America pays homage to men and women who served their country.

★　★　★
Echo
"Please accept this flag on behalf of the
President of the United States and a grateful nation."

For many widows, their husband's military funeral is the first one they have attended. The solemnity and formality of the ceremony can make it appear surreal. Some widows feel disconnected from the service, as if they are watching someone else's life. Others go through the motions like a robot. People often mistake this fragile composure of the widow as a sign that she is doing okay, when nothing could be further from the truth.

Some widows don't remember too much about the funeral; for others, every detail is seared into their memory. Most widows fall somewhere in between. All would have preferred not to bury their young husbands.

★ ★ ★
Lessons Learned
The time-honored traditions of a military funeral
are a fitting tribute to your husband
but hard on you as a military wife made widow.

THE MEMORIAL SERVICE

Your husband's command most likely had a memorial service for him. This service is usually held after the funeral and can be just as formal as a military funeral. Once again, the traditions of your husband's service branch were followed, from the Final Roll Call for fallen Soldiers to the Missing Man flyby for aviators. Many widows have found these ceremonies and rituals incredibly poignant but, at the same time, emotionally devastating.

You may have found yourself in the position where more than one memorial service was held for your husband, with additional services held at previous duty stations, schools or colleges, or in his hometown. You probably appreciated the tributes paid to your husband, but if you attended several services, you may have become burned out by them. This is a normal reaction, a grief overload, so don't feel guilty.

★ ★ ★
Echo
"As the memorial service ended, it started to rain,
and all I could think was that God was crying with me."

THE PUBLIC NATURE OF A MILITARY DEATH

Deaths in the military are public events. Even before the official word is out, the media can be intrusive and relentless, pursuing you, your family, your friends and neighbors, and even your coworkers. If you were living on base when your husband was killed, we hope the PAO (Public Affairs Office) protected you from the media frenzy. If you were living off base, there was a good chance you found the media camped out on your lawn, and you and your family were besieged whenever you opened the door. The PAO can help you with the press, no matter where you live.

If your husband dies in the military, you may appreciate the public recognition and sympathy, but it may be hard to share your personal pain with the rest of the world. You never imagined your everyday life or your husband's death would end up as a thirty-second sound bite on the evening news. Unfortunately, his death was probably just the beginning of the news coverage. The press was likely present at your husband's funeral and the memorial service, focusing on you as his widow and capturing on film the worst moments of your life.

★ ★ ★

Lesson Learned
A military death is a public event. Privacy is a luxury.

MILITARY CEMETERIES

Some widows find comfort in going to the cemetery. Others do not; for them, visiting their husband's grave is an unnerving event. Either way, if you buried your husband in Arlington National Cemetery or any other veterans cemetery, you know that they are quite different from those in the civilian community.

In a civilian cemetery, there is a wide variety of headstones, in an array of sizes and shapes. In a military cemetery, however, there is row after row of similar tombstones laid out with military precision in crisp lines and perfect columns. These tombstones seem to stand watch over the graves of their fallen brothers in arms. From a distance, they all look alike. But each one is unique; each stone tells the short life history of the special person who is buried beneath. It is hard to believe that just a few feet of dirt separate you from your husband.

★ ★ ★

Lesson Learned
It's a sobering slice of reality
to see your husband's name on a tombstone.

AUTOPSY AND INVESTIGATION REPORTS

In almost all cases, when your husband's body was recovered, the military performed an autopsy to determine the cause of his death. You had no say in whether or not the autopsy was performed, and that might have disturbed you. But it is a part of the military's procedures for investigating active duty deaths. We hope the examination of your husband's body was done in a timely manner, one that didn't result in too long a delay in the funeral arrangements.

An autopsy report is a clinical document. As a layperson, even after reading this report, you still may not have completely understood how your husband died. This may have frustrated you if you hoped this report would have shed light on the exact cause of his death.

★ ★ ★

Lesson Learned
You may never know exactly how your husband died.

If your husband was killed in an accident or mishap, the military probably conducted at least one, and probably two, investigations. These were done to determine the cause of the accident and to identify corrective actions to prevent it from reoccurring. Just as in civilian accident investigations, the last actions of the deceased are thoroughly scrutinized.

As part of the investigation, you were probably asked some very personal questions about your husband's last hours and days, including his food and alcohol consumption, your sex life, and his mood when he left the house. At a time when you were already upset, these questions may have seemed very intrusive. We agree, but your answers can provide some information that may be important to the accident investigation.

A frustrating situation arises when you yearn for the details of your husband's last moments of life, yet the military, in the midst of an investigation, provides you with little information. We understand your crucial need to know what happened. We also understand the military's reluctance to release preliminary findings that may prove to be incorrect. The military is making great strides to find the balance between providing you with the answers you seek and preserving the integrity of the investigation until it is finished.

THE PRESENCE OF ONGOING REMINDERS

NATIONAL HOLIDAYS

With the death of someone we love, there are untold reminders that connect us to that person and remind us of our loss. These can be subtle or obvious, and they often inflict unexpected distress. Because your husband was in the military, these reminders often come on a national scale.

Let's start with the national holidays of Memorial Day and Veterans Day. Before your husband died, you probably thought of Memorial Day as a three-day weekend at the end of May and the unofficial start of summer. Like many people in America, you probably did not fully understand that Memorial Day is set aside to honor our nation's war dead. Likewise, Veterans Day in November is a national holiday to honor all military veterans. On both of these holidays, our nation pauses to remember military veterans, living and dead, with parades and ceremonies of recognition and thanks.

Your husband's death in the military probably changed the way you view Memorial Day and Veterans Day. While you still socialize and shop the sales on these holidays, you have come to realize that these national days of remembrance now reflect your husband's sacrifice.

MILITARY CONNECTIONS

If you still shop in the commissary or the PX (post exchange), you know that trips to these stores can open up a floodgate of emotions. Every uniform you see is a reminder of your husband. Every uniformed serviceman is shopping with his wife and family, but you are alone. Seeing unit patches and insignia on uniforms can be upsetting and reduce you to tears.

If you live near a military installation, you are likely to see the tanks he rode in, the Humvees he drove, the helicopters he piloted, and the planes he flew. You may be haunted by these pieces of military hardware because they now represent symbols of your husband's death, where before they were just familiar equipment. Even if you don't live near a military base, you will see these glaring reminders on television and in movies. They have always been there, but now they leap out at you as another connection to your military husband's death.

★ ★ ★
Echo
"I can't bear to see homecomings on the news anymore.
They remind me that my husband came home in a casket."

CONTINUING TIES TO THE MILITARY SYSTEM

The magic number to everything in the military is your husband's SSN. Whether your husband is dead or alive, he remains your sponsor in the eyes of DEERS (the Defense Enrollment Eligibility Reporting System), which is the database of military sponsors and their families who are entitled to military benefits. As long as you are unmarried, you will be your husband's dependent.

Because you are still considered his dependent, each time you use military benefits or services that require his name and status, you will end up explaining that you are a widow—and the story that goes along with it. Renewing the base decal for your vehicle can turn into a major emotional production if the clerk insists you must register your car in your husband's name and give his duty station and duty phone number. Arlington National Cemetery is not considered a duty station, however permanent it is.

Simple actions and transactions on base, such as paying by check, can force you to face your widowed status repeatedly. Even a trip to a civilian doctor necessitates that you list your dead husband as your sponsor on the insurance forms.

These simple tasks of daily living can become significant emotional events when you must continually retell how you became a widow. Like other widows before you, you may have wondered if the system will ever give you a break by letting your husband and his SSN rest in peace.

★ ★ ★

Echo
"The 'DEC' on my ID card stands for 'deceased,' not 'December.'"

PUTTING IT ALL TOGETHER

As we have pointed out, the military culture has a tremendous impact on your grief. It starts with how you learned of your husband's death and continues as you adjust to the "new normal" world as a military widow. When you take your life experiences, combine them with how and why your husband died, and wrap the culture of the military around them, you have a more complete picture of why military widowhood is complex.

PART THREE

When Your Husband Dies Suddenly

CHAPTER 6

★ ★ ★

TYPES OF DEATH:
ANTICIPATED VERSUS SUDDEN

Glen and Annie

Glen and Annie loved being stationed at Kadena AFB in Okinawa, where they could fly "space available" all over the Far East. They recently went to Tokyo and looked forward to a shopping trip to Korea in the spring.

Glen was a master sergeant and flight line supervisor. He had a reputation as a go-getter who would help out wherever he was needed. Right after lunch one Monday, Glen was overseeing the unloading of cargo from a transient KC-10. As the K-loader pulled away from the aircraft, Glen lost his balance and fell through the open cargo door to the ramp.

Glen was taken to the base hospital. Unable to breathe on his own, Glen was put on a mechanical ventilator. All indications were that he had broken his neck. The doctors were not optimistic about his chances of survival.

Annie kept vigil at Glen's bedside throughout the night. Further testing and consultation with specialists showed that Glen had no remaining brain function. After talking with the doctors and the hospital chaplain, Annie authorized the staff to take Glen off life support. In what little private time she had with Glen, Annie could not tell him all that she wanted to say.

Just a few weeks before his accident, Glen had signed an organ donor card, and Annie arranged with the physicians to honor his wishes. She felt that some good could come out of Glen's death. He was always helping others, and even in death, Glen would continue to do so.

When Annie was finally taken back to their home, she found Glen's note from the previous morning, asking her to pick up a new oil filter for the car. She stared at his handwriting, not believing that Glen was dead. Yesterday, one of her tasks was to buy an oil filter. Today, she needed to start thinking about burying her husband.

*U*P TO THIS POINT IN YOUR LIFE, you probably haven't given much thought to how people die. But, it makes a difference. How your husband died affects not only how you responded to the news of his death, but also how you work through the tasks of grief.

Deaths are divided into two general categories: anticipated and sudden. We will describe some of the dynamics of each.

ANTICIPATED DEATHS

Anticipated deaths occur when a person is terminally ill, and his or her physical condition has deteriorated to the point where there is no hope of recovery. In other words, death is inevitable. Most anticipated deaths are due to disease or illness.

For example, if your husband had terminal cancer, his body became a battlefield, often with long and lengthy battles fought between human resilience and an aggressive disease. You knew your husband was going to die in the near future. You didn't want to lose him, and although you always maintained hope of a cure or a miracle, you knew it was just a matter of time. You anticipated your husband's death as the last phase of his illness.

If your husband suffered greatly, you may have felt relief when his pain was finally over. Still, it is extremely difficult to watch your husband die slowly. In all likelihood, you did not come to grips with his death until he died and your feelings of relief that his suffering was over began to subside. Only then did you truly feel the pain of losing him.

With an anticipated death, you may have blamed your husband for not taking better care of his health. Or perhaps you blamed yourself for not recognizing his symptoms earlier and insisting he get medical treatment.

SUDDEN DEATHS

Sudden deaths occur without forewarning. Neither the deceased nor the survivors are aware that death is just around the corner.

If your husband died suddenly, you were not prepared—his death was a shock to your body and psyche. Your ability to cope with the news and the immediate aftermath was compromised. Sudden death robbed you of the chance to say good-bye, to exchange words of love or forgiveness, to tend to unfinished business, and to begin to prepare for a world without him.

There are two types of sudden death: natural and human caused.

NATURAL SUDDEN DEATHS

Some sudden deaths happen due to natural causes, such as heart attacks, strokes, or aneurysms. If your husband died suddenly from a natural cause, you had no time to prepare emotionally or practically. One moment he was alive and healthy, and the next, your world was filled with hospitals, doctors and nurses, medical tests, intravenous tubes, and fear. Even if your husband lived for a few days afterward, his death was still sudden to you. You were likely left stunned and shaken by the unexpectedness and finality of his departure.

Other sudden deaths occur because of natural disasters—sometimes called "acts of God"—such as tornadoes, earthquakes, floods, hurricanes, and typhoons. With this form of natural sudden death, the actions are happening *to* the body, not from *within* the body. If your husband died as a result of a natural disaster, he may have been in some danger before losing the battle to Mother Nature.

With natural sudden deaths, you may be angry with the medical staff for not doing more to save your husband. Or you may blame God for allowing this natural disaster to occur.

HUMAN-CAUSED SUDDEN DEATHS

The second category of sudden deaths is those caused by people. These include war and terrorism, accidents, homicides, and suicides. The death of someone you love is always heartbreaking, but when your husband was killed by the actions of another person, it is especially devastating.

If your husband died in this manner, your grief most likely will be complex and intense. This type of sudden death, sometimes called traumatic death, demands more from you than the normal grief responses to an anticipated or natural death.

Grief expert Therese Rando (1993) described some general conditions that define a death as traumatic. Not every condition must be present for the death to be traumatic to you. According to Dr. Rando, traumatic deaths are

- sudden and unexpected,
- random or preventable,
- violent, with damage to and possibly dismemberment of the body,
- one of multiple deaths that occurred at the same time, and
- a significant threat to your own survival, or
- the "shocking confrontation with the death or mutilation of others."

★ ★ ★

Echo

"The fact that my husband's death was preventable still angers me to this very day."

Combat, combat-related, and training deaths—which are all forms of sudden, traumatic death—are especially hard on military widows. These deaths usually cause significant damage to the body, often making it non-viewable or non-recoverable.

A traumatic death can take its toll on you from the moment you receive notification. The physical and emotional shock may handicap you, making you so overwhelmed by the news that you withdraw emotionally to avoid the pain.

Traumatic death may leave you preoccupied with the circumstances of your husband's death, a strong need to make sense of it, and often an obsession to determine blame, affix responsibility, and demand punishment or retribution. With sudden, traumatic deaths, you will most likely be angry with an individual, an organization, a terrorist group, or an entire nation.

This all makes sense, according to Dr. Rando (1993); the more violent or brutal the death, the more intense will be the "anxiety, fear, violation, powerlessness, and, ultimately, anger, guilt, self-blame and shattered assumptions" that mourners will face afterward.

★ ★ ★

Lesson Learned

How and why your husband died has a great impact on your grief.

PUTTING IT ALL TOGETHER

The way in which your husband died does make a difference. It can affect how you responded to the news of his death and how you deal with it over time. If your husband was ill before he died, even the knowledge of his pending death was not enough to soften the blow.

Sudden deaths, especially traumatic deaths, are common in the military, and usually add a different dimension of anguish to your loss. You are faced not only with the shock of your husband's death, but also with the way in which he died.

CHAPTER 7

★　★　★

MYTHS ABOUT GRIEF

Jimmy and Carla

When Jimmy and Carla first met in their early thirties, they hit it off right away. The more they talked, the more they found they had a lot in common. Both were from poor families and knew what it was like to live paycheck to paycheck. All his life, Jimmy dreamed of one day owning his own landscaping business in their hometown of Beaumont, Texas. Carla shared this dream with Jimmy, and after they were married, they both worked hard and saved to make it happen.

Jimmy, a sergeant first class in the Army, was three years away from retirement when he got orders to a heavy engineer battalion in Hanau, Germany. Carla had a good-paying job in Beaumont that she was reluctant to give up. It would help their retirement dreams if she continued to work and bank her paycheck. Jimmy and Carla had a big decision to make. As hard as living apart would be for them, Jimmy went to Germany unaccompanied.

One Wednesday morning, about a year into his tour, Jimmy didn't report for duty. He was later found dead in his quarters. His body was taken to the Army's Landstuhl Regional Medical Center, where the autopsy revealed his death was from heart failure. Although Jimmy was slightly overweight, he never reported any alarming symptoms.

After Jimmy died, Carla couldn't help but wish she had gone to Germany with him. Her reason for remaining behind—the extra money—now seemed hollow. She felt that had she gone with Jimmy, she surely would have noticed some unusual symptoms that, treated early, could have prevented his death.

Because of her father's death, Carla thought she knew a lot about grief. But she was quite surprised at how hard Jimmy's death hit her. Carla found she couldn't work because her concentration was so poor. She spent the first six months after her husband's death sitting on her sofa, mindlessly watching the afternoon soap operas. After the first year, Carla was sure something was wrong with her; she expected to be feeling much better. After all, other people had losses and they didn't seem as strongly affected as she was.

Carla heard about a grief workshop near her house and decided to attend. The very first night, she was relieved to learn that many of her reactions to losing Jimmy were quite common. She made an instant connection with another widow, and they often met outside the group.

*b*ECAUSE THIS MAY BE YOUR FIRST EXPERIENCE with the death of someone close to you, you may not know much about grief—nor did you want to learn about it this way. Perhaps your only knowledge of grief comes from the movies, where, typically, a bereaved widow bravely faces the future and turns her life around in two short, made-for-television hours. As you are finding out, however, real life is much different from the movies.

To help you understand that what you feel is normal—and you are *not* going crazy—we would like to dispel some common myths about grief.

MYTH: WE ALL GRIEVE THE SAME WAY

While we all experience common elements of grief, each of our losses is mourned differently because every loss is unique. We have different grief reactions, depending on the nature and closeness of the lost relationship.

This is also true for you, and the relationship you had with your husband. How you grieve his loss depends on a number of factors. Among these are the quality of your relationship with him, how he died and at what age, any previous losses you have had, how you coped with other trials in your life, your support system of friends and family members, and your religious beliefs and cultural background.

The integration of these factors personalized the relationship with your husband. Consequently, they also personalize your grief. Don't let anyone tell you how to grieve, or that you're going about it all wrong.

Myth: Grief Should Take Only One Year

There is no set time for the process of mourning, although the world will want you to be "over it" probably before you're ready. Family and friends will usually tolerate your sadness and tears for about a year, because that is the unofficial amount of time allotted to a grieving person. Even your closest friends and relatives may not understand that military grief is complicated and may take you longer to work through than one year.

Being told you should be "over it," according to someone else's time-table, can cause you additional stress. While others might think they are being helpful by nudging you to move on, they can unknowingly make you feel weak or incompetent or—worse—that you are failing at grief.

Myth: If I Keep Busy, I Can Get Through This Easier

A wise Navy chaplain once told us that, with grief, it is either "pay now or pay later." If you ignore it now, grief will inevitably catch up with you one day. You can try to avoid grief, but it will still be there, waiting for you when you least expect it. The only way to ease the pain is to work through it. To get to the other side of grief, you must embrace the feelings and mourn your loss. Difficult as it is to believe, grieving is the healthiest way to deal with the death of your husband.

Myth: Grief Is a Predictable and Orderly Series of Stages

Grief is made up of many emotions and reactions that we will discuss in chapter 8. These reactions and feelings do not progress in any logical or orderly fashion. You don't complete one stage and then move on to the next. Typically, you trudge through grief as though you are trying to walk through sticky, gooey mud. Because there is no checklist for grief, the process can be maddening, especially if you are a person who likes to cross things off your list when you have finished them.

Myth: Once You're Done with Grief, You're Done

If you think of grieving as a process, with ebbs and flows of emotion, you can understand how you might suddenly find yourself feeling sad or teary-eyed when you think about your husband even after years have passed. Grief expert Alan Wolfelt (1992) described these grief attacks as "memory embraces" or "grief spasms." These episodes are normal, even expected. However, they do not mean you are going back to the time when your grief was so overwhelming and painful.

Grief spasms seem to come out of nowhere. They may be triggered by something big, like hearing of a military death similar to your husband's, or something small, like eating his favorite food in a restaurant. They may also arise around significant dates in your relationship with your spouse. Don't be thrown by these episodes; they are a normal part of missing your husband. The good news is this: while these grief spasms can be painful, you will find they occur less frequently, are less intense, and are easier to recover from as time marches on.

Myth: Tears Are a Sign of Weakness

In fact, the opposite is true. The human body is designed to be resilient and to cope with whatever life deals out. Recent studies have supported this idea. They have shown that tears shed for different reasons contain different kinds of chemicals. Studies done by William Frey, a Minnesota biochemist, have shown that emotional tears contain more of the chemical by-products of stress hormones and natural painkillers than did tears shed after chopping onions (Skorucak, 2002).

So the next time you cry over your husband's death, remember that this is your body's way of getting rid of the by-products of stress and grief. Shedding tears is actually very healthy. Keep a box of tissues handy and don't hold back on these tears. You are doing important grief work, and you are on the way to becoming stronger and feeling better.

★ ★ ★

Lesson Learned

There is no short, orderly, or pain-free way through grief.

Putting It All Together

Grief may be a new experience for you. Learn as much accurate information about it as you can. This will help you understand that your reactions are shared by other widows. This knowledge will also show you the signposts along—and help you to map out the geography of—this unknown terrain called grief.

CHAPTER 8

★ ★ ★

COMMON GRIEF RESPONSES
TO LOSING YOUR HUSBAND

Travis and Wendy

Growing up in Winslow, Arizona, Travis and Wendy lived only a few miles apart but never met until they attended the same Bible study class. They were immediately attracted to each other and found they came from families that had significant emotional problems and could easily be labeled as dysfunctional. Travis and Wendy couldn't wait to move away from their families' craziness and start their lives together. The Coast Guard was their ticket out, and so Travis signed up.

When he and Wendy had been married about a year and a half, Travis, a seaman, received orders to the Coast Guard Shipyard in Curtis Bay, near Baltimore, Maryland. The couple moved to a small but cozy apartment off base, and they joined a local church whose members quickly became their new family. Wendy worked as a part-time clerk in a nearby convenience store and saved all this money in what they called the "baby fund."

One morning, Travis was off-loading material from a truck at a warehouse on base. The dock lock, a safety mechanism that holds the truck to the unloading dock, was not engaged, nor had the truck's wheels been chocked. Thinking the unloading process was finished, the truck driver pulled away from the dock. When the truck lurched forward, Travis's forklift fell off the back of the truck and overturned. His chest was crushed; Travis died instantly.

Travis's blood test, a normal part of the accident investigation, indicated no evidence of drugs or alcohol.

Wendy decided to bury Travis in Arizona. She doesn't remember too much about the funeral, nor does she want to. Being with their families again, Wendy realized she couldn't move back to Winslow, but she didn't know where she would like to live.

Wendy was encouraged not to make any major decisions for at least a year, and so she stayed in Maryland near her new friends at church. Her church had a weekly bereavement support group, and even though Wendy was the youngest widow there, she discovered quite a bit about her grief. She learned that many of her reactions to Travis's sudden death were very common. Because of what she learned in the grief group, Wendy stopped worrying that she was going crazy.

*Y*OU MAY HAVE EXPERIENCED OTHER LOSSES in your life prior to your husband's sudden death. But what you are finding now is that losing your husband is not like losing any other loved one. Your reactions are more intense, hurt with a greater depth, and last for a longer time. There is more upheaval in your life, and your day-to-day world has probably been reduced to a churning sea of disbelief, confusion, and turmoil.

In the late 1960s, Elisabeth Kübler-Ross, a physician and the author of *On Death and Dying* (1969), observed that people who were terminally ill went through the five emotional stages of denial, anger, bargaining, depression, and acceptance. Although these stages were never intended to define grief after a death, they became accepted as the stages of grief.

Grief experts now acknowledge that people do not go through stages of grief in a predictable order. Rather, people usually experience a wide range of reactions that may include denial, anger, bargaining, depression, and acceptance but are not limited to them. These responses do not happen in any sort of order. In fact, you most likely experience more than one reaction at the same time. Like the weather, your feelings may change completely in ten minutes. This is normal.

You may have thought that grief comes out only through tears and emotions. Grief will show up in your life in many ways, however. In addition to emotions, there are several other components to grief:

- Physical—how your body responds.
- Behavioral—how you act.
- Cognitive—how you think.
- Social—how you relate to others.
- Spiritual—how you find meaning in your husband's death.

Each component of grief is real. You need to be aware of each one as you work through your loss. Some components of grief will be troublesome for you, while others will be less difficult. Remember, you and your grief are unique.

Before we look at the components of grief, we want to examine some of the initial reactions you may have experienced to the news of your husband's death.

INITIAL REACTIONS

When your husband dies suddenly or is killed traumatically, extreme immediate responses are the norm. Initially, the news probably put you into a state of shock. You could not take in the thought that your husband was dead. It was unbelievable, difficult to comprehend, and unacceptable to even think about. Yet all around you, people behaved as though this horrifying news were true.

Upon hearing of your husband's death, any or all of the following reactions would be within the realm of normal. Some of these reactions may be quite intense, others might produce a fair to moderate response, and some may not occur at all.

- Denial of the news of your husband's death.
- Anger at the military officials notifying you.
- Horror over the details of your husband's death, especially if it was violent or traumatic.
- Aversion to hearing your husband described in the past tense or as "remains" or a "body."
- Frustration over the lack of information you're getting.
- Emotional numbness, which may be misunderstood as being emotionally in control.
- Uncontrollable sobbing, until you can't breathe.
- Isolation from family and friends who are far away.

These intense reactions will begin to subside, usually within days after you have been notified, and the funeral and memorial services are over.

★ ★ ★

Echo
"I thought that if I didn't talk to the casualty officer, my husband wouldn't be dead."

COMMON GRIEF REACTIONS

Do not be surprised as other feelings, thoughts, and behaviors that are broader in scope surface in the weeks and months ahead. This roller coaster of emotions will last for some time. It is a part of grief.

EMOTIONAL REACTIONS

Emotional reactions are the most obvious display of grief. They are what you feel first, and what people expect to see in a grieving widow. You will likely experience many emotional reactions. You may feel that you are caught up in a cyclone, a whirlwind of feelings and thoughts you are helpless to control. As your life circumstances change, so will your emotional responses.

Here are some emotional reactions experienced by other widows. Again, remember everyone is different, and there is no military regulation that requires you to feel them all.

- Continued denial—refusing to believe your husband's death happened.
- Yearning—intense longing for him.
- Depression—hopeless and helpless.
- Emptiness—feeling nothing inside.
- Fragility—everything upsets you.
- Feeling overwhelmed—even simple tasks are hard.
- Anger—at everything and everyone.
- Fear—scared of the days and weeks ahead.
- Guilt—regretting past words or actions.
- Relief—if he was abusive.
- Apprehension—about other bad things happening.
- Thoughts of death—not wanting to live anymore.

Emotions are an integral part of your grief. Yet, they may be frightening at times. Keep in mind that what is normal for you may be an extreme response for someone else. These emotional reactions will not always be constant but will ebb and flow like the ocean tides.

PHYSICAL REACTIONS

Perhaps you didn't realize there is a distinct physical side to grief. While you may experience a wide range of physical reactions, don't assume that all of them are normal—always check with your doctor. Some physical symptoms are caused by other problems not related to grief. For example, if you don't eat, your brain is not getting the nourishment it needs, and you may have headaches or can't think straight. You are also under a lot of stress, and this can easily cause you to feel mentally, physically, and emotionally exhausted.

Here are some of the more common physical reactions to grief:
- Changes in sleep patterns—too little, too much, or disturbed sleep.
- Changes in appetite—not eating enough, overeating, or eating the wrong foods.
- Loss of energy—fatigued and often exhausted.
- Restlessness—need to keep moving and "do something."
- Anxiety and panic attacks—catastrophic fear and hyperventilation.
- Backaches, neck aches, or headaches—heightened tension.
- Gastrointestinal problems—constipation, diarrhea, or upset stomach.
- Changes in sexual interest—decreased or increased feelings of sexuality.
- Susceptibility to illness—often getting sick.
- Dry mouth—metallic taste or cotton mouth.
- Sighing—for no reason.
- "The Look"—blank facial expression.

It is important to remember that grief can have a significant adverse effect on your body. Have any physical symptoms checked out by your doctor. You do not need to suffer, and your physical health is too important to neglect.

BEHAVIORAL REACTIONS

With all the upheaval in your life, you may find yourself acting in ways that are out of character. In fact, you may not even realize you're behaving differently until someone points it out. Don't shoot the messenger. Your family and friends have your best interests at heart, and they do not want to see you act in unhealthy or destructive ways. Here are some behaviors you and your family should watch out for:

- Trying to escape the pain in unhealthy ways—drinking too much alcohol, using illegal drugs, or misusing prescription medications.
- Lacking the desire to eat—skipping meals or eating poorly.
- Spending days on the sofa or unable to get out of bed— an indication of depression.
- Neglecting your personal appearance—not caring how you look.
- Screaming and cursing—sometimes out of control.
- Pacing back and forth—unable to stay still.
- Taking care of others—easier to focus on them and avoid you.
- "Seeing" your husband—following other men or a familiar car.
- Acting out—behaving in ways that are out of character for you.

Your behavior is sometimes an indication of what is going on inside. Extreme behaviors can hurt you, your kids, and those with whom you come in contact. They have a way of making a bad situation worse. Find a person you can trust to talk out any changes in your behavior.

COGNITIVE REACTIONS

You may have difficulty thinking clearly, handling simple tasks, or solving problems. This can be scary, especially if you were organized before your husband died. Keep in mind that you are not losing it. Rather, you are experiencing the component of grief that affects your ability to think. It is common to have your thought processes impaired by grief. Here are some general cognitive reactions experienced by widows:

- No concentration—can't stay focused on anything.
- Loss of memory—forgetting names, places, dates, and appointments.
- Can't think straight—unable to sort out your thoughts.

- Obsessive thoughts—continually thinking about your husband's death.
- Disorganized—can't get anything done.
- Questioning—"How will I survive without him? How can I go on?"
- Pretending he is still alive—easier to live in a dream world.

It is especially frustrating, and a bit frightening, when you can't think straight. You are not alone in feeling this way; many other widows struggle with muddled thoughts and difficulty concentrating. Once again, go easy on yourself, and don't be afraid to ask for help.

SOCIAL REACTIONS

Most widows do not initially realize there is a social aspect to grief. Perhaps you have already found out that your relationships with others were affected by your husband's death. You are no longer the "old you," and your needs and reasons to connect with people are different. You may not have any interest in your usual activities, or you may find you don't have the energy to pursue them. Often, it's easier to stay home alone. Here are a few social reactions widows have experienced:

- Abandonment—close friends become distant without explanation.
- Isolation—withdrawing from others.
- Neediness—depending on others more than you did before.
- Labeled "the widow"—your identity is defined by your husband's death.

The social changes of widowhood can be especially distressing. You are already hurting and feeling vulnerable, and when family, friends, and even strangers treat you differently, it may seem like another unnecessary burden has been placed on your shoulders.

SPIRITUAL REACTIONS

Many fundamental spiritual questions arise after your husband dies. His death will likely shake your most basic beliefs about life, death, religion, spirituality, and the nature and role of God in your life. For some women, the sudden death of their husband propels them into a crisis of faith. Other women find great comfort and strength in their faith in God, and within their faith community. Many widows fall somewhere in between.

One thing is certain: whatever your religious beliefs, the death of your husband will likely launch you on a journey of spiritual searching and a quest to find meaning in his death, and possibly in your own life.

Here are a few of the many possible spiritual reactions you might have to your husband's death:

- Asking why—"Why . . . why . . . why?"
- Wondering if there is life after death—"Is my husband all right wherever he is?"
- Wondering if there is a heaven—"Does he live on in a spiritual form?"
- Being angry at God—"Why did you let this happen?"

There are many more difficult questions, with no easy answers. In all likelihood, your search for spiritual understanding will keep you awake many nights. We urge you not to skip over this important component of grief. This spiritual journey may take some time, but it can help you get through the darkest hours. It is worth the search for some peace of mind.

★ ★ ★

Lesson Learned
Grief affects every part of who you are.

PUTTING IT ALL TOGETHER

In this chapter, we have gone over the six components of grief: the emotional, physical, behavioral, cognitive, social, and spiritual pieces. In reality, many of these pieces of grief overlap and are intertwined with each other. They create reactions within you that are sometimes confusing and misunderstood. Don't expect to place your feelings, thoughts, and actions into one neat and tidy category.

We hope you have a better understanding of what makes up your grief, and why you feel, think, and act the way you do.

CHAPTER 9

★ ★ ★

GRIEF WORK

Brian and Madison

Brian had been a member of the New Jersey National Guard for thirteen years. When his infantry battalion was federally activated and received orders to Iraq for a year, his wife, Madison, had a feeling of dread. She had this gut feeling that Brian wouldn't come home alive. She shared her fears with the Family Readiness Group at the National Guard Armory, and the wives in the group encouraged her to keep a positive attitude. Each passing day meant a day closer to his return. Once they passed the six-month mark of the deployment, Madison's fears lessened, and she started to plan for Brian's homecoming.

Over in Iraq, Brian did see some hostile action, but most of his time was spent driving a HMMWV (high mobility multipurpose wheeled vehicle), what civilians call a jeep. One Sunday evening, in the midst of a particularly intense and blinding dust storm near Karbala, Brian's HMMWV swerved to avoid an Iraqi tractor trailer and rolled over into a drainage ditch. All three Soldiers in the HMMWV drowned.

Back in New Jersey, Madison's premonition—that Brian wasn't coming home alive—came true. While she feared that Brian would be killed in combat, Madison never dreamed he would drown in the middle of a desert. She felt she could better accept Brian's death if he had died in combat, but Madison couldn't get past the fact that Brian died in a nonhostile accident.

While watching a popular afternoon talk show, Madison caught a segment on military widowhood. She was riveted; she felt the talk show host and her guests were talking about her. As she listened, Madison realized there were other women in America who felt just as she did. She knew little about grief, and even less about military widowhood. She was relieved to hear that military grief is often complex because she was afraid that something was wrong with her. The show gave Madison a profound sense of hope.

Verses 1 through 8 of chapter 3 in the Old Testament book of Ecclesiastes (New American Bible, 1990) tell us

There is an appointed time for everything and
a time for every affair under the heavens.
A time to be born, and a time to die; . . .
A time to weep, and a time to laugh;
A time to mourn, and a time to dance; . . .
A time to embrace, and a time to be far from embraces; . . .
A time to love, and a time to hate;
A time of war, and a time of peace.

*t*HIS IS YOUR TIME TO MOURN AND GRIEVE. Because you loved your husband, you will feel the sorrow and anguish of his death. This is called grief. The only way to get past this intense grief is to go through it. It takes work. It is hard and painful, but it is necessary. You didn't fall in love with your husband in a day, and you cannot mourn his death in a day or two either.

Working through grief is like walking through mud. Each step is an effort, and progress is measured in inches, not miles. Like mud, grief is messy. By the end of the day, you're covered in it from head to toe, and should you stumble and fall, it's downright embarrassing. When you're stuck in the mud, you want to give up and quit. But, the only way to get through the muck and mire is to keep moving forward. The same goes for grief.

We cannot teach you how to grieve, but we can outline some tasks to help you lessen the burden and feel better about yourself and life again. There is a long-standing belief that "time heals all wounds." In fact, we believe that time heals nothing. The healing comes from doing grief work. Time provides you with the opportunity.

Grief counselor and educator Alan Wolfelt (2003) has identified these six needs of mourning to help people work through grief:

- You accept the reality of your husband's death.
- You let yourself feel the pain of the loss.
- You remember your husband.
- You develop a new self-identity.
- You search for meaning in your husband's death.
- You let others help you.

The following pages describe what you need to know about each of these needs.

You Accept the Reality of Your Husband's Death

Just because you were officially notified and went through the motions of burying your husband's remains does not necessarily mean you fully believe, much less accept, that his death really occurred. It may take you many months or sometimes a year or two to fully admit that your husband is dead.

The truth is that reality comes in small slices and invades your life in normal, everyday ways. It's a slice of reality when you realize your husband's toothbrush has not been used in months. Or you reach for your cell phone to call him, momentarily forgetting he will not be on the other end. How reality hits home is different for each widow. But each instance brings the message that your husband is dead.

★ ★ ★

Echo
*"Even though I knew my husband was gone,
I didn't want to move, because I kept thinking
he wouldn't know my new address or phone number."*

Perhaps you have an almost obsessive need to talk about your husband, how he died, the condition of his remains, or the details of his funeral. While your family and friends may find this morbid, talking about your husband and his death makes it a little more real. You may find you can say that your husband is not coming home again, but you can't get the "D" word out of your mouth. Some widows dance around using the "D" word for a very long time. It is an emotional and sobering moment the first time you say, "My husband is dead."

Many widows can remember the very day they first used those words. When you actually say your husband is dead, you are not only admitting that he's gone, but also that he's not coming back. Accepting this fact is an important step in your grief work.

It is an agonizing trip through reality's field of mud, but a necessary one for you to make. No doubt you will trip and fall a few times as you are caught off guard by the smallest reminders of your husband. Each step is progress, though, and you are headed in the right direction.

★　★　★
Lesson Learned
It takes a long time for your heart to accept
what your head has been told.

YOU LET YOURSELF FEEL THE PAIN OF THE LOSS

You do not stop loving your husband when he dies, and sorrow is what you feel when you lose someone you love. As you know, the depth and breadth of this pain can feel endless. At times, you ache emotionally and physically. It is as if every fiber and nerve of your body hurts. Simply said, it can be excruciating.

★　★　★
Echo
"A part of me died with my husband on that god-awful
day he was killed. In the deep despair that shrouded the weeks and
months after he died, pieces of me died again and again
as I faced the bitter reality of his death.
Yet each morning I woke up, condemned to live another day."

No one looks forward to feeling pain, especially of this nature and type. The intensity will not last, but it's necessary for you to feel it and work through it. Living through this pain can be exhausting, and you will need to take breaks and recharge your battery. One widow we know scheduled a massage for herself every week—her way of revitalizing herself. Taking a breather from grief does not mean you love your husband less. Don't avoid it completely, though—grief will not go away on its own.

Our society does not like to see people grieve, so your family and friends may encourage you to be strong and not give in to the tears and sadness. Don't let anyone talk you out of the opportunity to grieve for your husband, or to receive the emotional support that comes with being newly widowed. In fact, put a box of tissues in each room of your home and two boxes in your car. You car is a great place to have a good cry. Tears are an expression of sorrow, so let them flow freely. Crying is a part of your grief work.

★　★　★

Lesson Learned
Pain and sorrow are the price of a love lost to death.

YOU REMEMBER YOUR HUSBAND

It is inconceivable to imagine that you will forget your husband. You shared the bonds of love and marriage, and his early death has an enormous impact on you. Cherish your memories of him—no new ones can be created. What is important is how you honor his memory, without being stuck in the past. Your husband's memory can and should have an appropriate place in your life, yet allow you to live in the present and plan for the future.

We all have the tendency to make our dead loved ones into saints. While it's good to remember the positive aspects of their personalities and lives, we need to have realistic memories: the good and bad times, his strengths and shortcomings, the traits you loved in him and those you found annoying. Your memory of your husband should be one of a real person.

It can be painful to convert your marriage from an earthly one of husband and wife to a relationship of memory and spirit. As part of your grief work, however, you must begin to loosen the emotional bonds to your husband. It is not easy to let go of someone you love. But it's something you must do, because your husband is no longer a part of your physical world.

Know that the memory of your husband lives on in large and small ways. Many military men often have public memorials dedicated to them, or buildings, streets, and parks named in their honor. If you have children, you will notice even more of their father in them, both now and as they grow into adulthood. Remember, too, that you can't be married without taking on some of your spouse's traits, likes, and habits. Your husband has influenced you in many ways. A part of him lives on.

★ ★ ★

Lesson Learned
*Honor your husband's memory in healthy and
life-affirming ways, yet live in the present.*

YOU DEVELOP A NEW SELF-IDENTITY

You have been forced into a new life you didn't want. No woman wants to be a widow; no one volunteers for this role. When your husband died, the part of you that was his wife died with him. This is a secondary loss. Something you enjoyed—your role as his wife—was taken away from you.

Another secondary loss unique to military widows is the loss of your military lifestyle. While you are still a military dependent, you are no longer the spouse of a service member, and your affiliation with your husband's command or unit will usually fade away. Your identity as a military spouse was defined by your husband.

We have heard widowhood described as a journey from wife to widow to woman. It makes sense to us and, we hope, to you, too. When you were first widowed, and for some time afterward, you still thought of yourself as your husband's wife. You felt like a wife and thought like one, too. You most likely wore your wedding ring and thought of yourself as a married woman. As the reality of widowhood slowly sank in, your identity transitioned from wife to widow. Quite a few military widows spend considerable time in this stage, where their identity is defined by widowhood. A few get stuck there and don't move on to become women in their own right again.

When you see yourself as a woman again, you will be a vastly different person from the woman you used to be. You will always be your husband's widow, but your whole identity is not defined by it. You are a woman who was changed in many ways, some of which you are not aware of yet.

★ ★ ★

Echo

"Yesterday I was a Soldier's wife. Who am I today?"

As part of your new self-identity, you must change from a "we" to an "I" mode of thinking. Even if you were accustomed to being alone because of your husband's deployment cycles, you were still a part of a couple. Now, all the responsibility of running the household and raising the kids falls on your shoulders, all the time.

Your new identity, however, is more than your roles, responsibilities, and the pieces of your married self that you lost. You cannot get through widowhood without being changed. Many widows like the changes they see in themselves, finding they are more patient, tolerant, and compassionate. They do not worry about insignificant things—they don't "sweat the small stuff" anymore!

YOU SEARCH FOR MEANING IN YOUR HUSBAND'S DEATH

Because your husband died young, you will probably search for the meaning behind his death in several ways. You will look for the physical cause of his death and try to understand what happened to him and how he died. You may or may not find the answers you seek; sometimes that happens with war, accidents, homicides, and suicides. Nonetheless, it is important to search for the details.

On another level, you will find yourself trying to comprehend his death in terms of the big questions of life. You may wonder what purpose his short life had, and why he died when he did. Like most young widows, you are finding that the death of your husband flies in the face of all your expectations about life.

In this trying time of emotional and spiritual wounding, you will likely reexamine the tough questions about the meaning of life and death. As part of this questioning, you will also try to figure out the purpose of your own life. You will likely rethink all you know about the world in order to come to a new understanding of it, one that makes sense of death and yet provides hope that a happy, meaningful future is possible.

Sometimes there is no single, easy answer to your search for meaning. In searching, though, you will find ways to live peacefully with the answers you have and to regain control over your life.

★   ★   ★

Lesson Learned

Some questions cannot be answered fully in this lifetime.

YOU LET OTHERS HELP YOU

The loss you feel after your husband dies is very personal and reflects the relationship you had with him. No one will feel the depth and pain of your loss in quite the same way you do because grief, like the relationship with your husband, is unique and personal.

While grief is a solitary journey in many ways, we encourage you not to go it alone. You have already sought help by reading this book. Asking for help from others is a sign of strength and a hope for a better tomorrow.

There are understanding, supportive people who will not try to fix your grief, but they will aid you in your grief work and support you along the way. They can be professionals—counselors, social workers, therapists, or nurses—or people who have experienced a loss themselves and understand the unique needs of military widows.

Do not be afraid to reach out to others through counseling, support groups, or connecting with other military widows. Having their support will help lessen your feelings of isolation, abandonment, and loneliness. All you can lose are your feelings of sorrow and loss. What you gain are encouragement, support, and a chance to feel better.

★   ★   ★

Lesson Learned

Getting help from other people can make your grief work easier.

PUTTING IT ALL TOGETHER

Grief work isn't easy, but neither is being a military widow. As we have emphasized, military grief is complex and therefore takes a long time to work through. Sometimes it seems like your grief will never end. When you feel this way, look back and see how far you have come. You will be surprised at how much progress you have already made. Remember that progress is measured in small steps rather than giant leaps.

CHAPTER 10

★ ★ ★

AM I GOING CRAZY?

Andy and Laura

Laura's pregnancy wasn't planned, so it took her and her husband, Andy, some time to get used to the idea. After the initial shock wore off, however, they were excited about becoming parents.

During Laura's last trimester, Andy, a Navy SEAL, deployed to the Middle East in support of Operation Iraqi Freedom. While Laura was accustomed to having Andy deploy, the hormonal imbalance of pregnancy wreaked havoc with her emotions. Despite Andy's assurances that he was well trained and nothing would happen to him, for the first time in their marriage Laura feared she would never see Andy alive again. Unfortunately, her fear became reality. While participating in a combat operation in the vicinity of Al Asad, Andy was fatally wounded by small-arms fire. Andy and Laura would never enjoy becoming parents together.

Laura was in her thirty-fifth week of pregnancy when Andy was killed. Just after she was notified, Laura started to have premature labor pains. The doctor hospitalized her to help Laura carry the baby to term. Even with constant monitoring, Laura went into early labor. She delivered a healthy five-pound baby girl six days after Andy died. She named her Olivia, the name they had picked out before Andy left for Iraq.

Andy's funeral had been postponed until Laura had the baby. Ignoring the advice of both families, Laura took her newborn infant to the funeral service. She wanted to be able to tell Olivia when she grew up that she was at her father's funeral.

Laura had a hard time adjusting. In just seven days—one week—she became both a widow and a mother. Each circumstance is life changing, but together they left Laura feeling like she was hanging on by her fingernails. She struggled with her constantly changing moods. The joy of becoming a mother was overshadowed by losing Andy. Laura found little delight in her baby, realizing that Andy was missing each new day in Olivia's life.

Laura discovered she couldn't stand to watch the news. Each story of another casualty made her relive Andy's death and reduced her to uncontrollable tears. These fatalities were more than news to Laura because she connected with the unknown new widows who now walked in her shoes.

Her obstetrician recognized that Laura's hormonal changes, in combination with the stress of Andy's death, created mood swings beyond what new mothers normally experience. She referred Laura to a therapist who specialized in traumatic loss.

*W*HEN THE SUN FINALLY SETS on the horror of talking with your casualty officer about non-viewable remains, funeral options, Social Security benefits, and SGLI (Servicemembers' Group Life Insurance) beneficiaries, and you are alone for the first time in days, you will probably wonder if you are going crazy. This is understandable; you have been thrown into the world of sudden, traumatic military death. There seems to be no escape or relief from it.

This type of death can assault every nerve and fiber within your body. You are probably experiencing extreme emotions that are downright scary. You may feel you have lost your grip on life. You are not alone with these feelings—ask any other widow you know. You are not going crazy, however; you are bereaved.

★ ★ ★
Echo
"This nightmare that invaded my life consumed my days and tormented my nights. I could not believe that my husband would never come home to me again."

You may have wondered whether you need counseling. Perhaps a friend or a relative has even suggested that you talk with someone, implying that you need to see a counselor or therapist. The real question, however, is not, "Do I need counseling?" but rather, "How can counseling help me?"

Some people think that going to a counselor means they are weak or crazy. Actually, the opposite is true. It is a sign of sanity to recognize that you are drowning in the deep end of the pool of grief. It takes personal strength to reach for a lifeline. These grief lifelines come in many forms, and we will tell you about some that are available, starting with counseling.

How Counseling Can Help You

YOUR HUSBAND'S DEATH WAS UNEXPECTED OR TRAUMATIC

You know all too well how difficult it has been to deal with a sudden and traumatic death. You look around and notice that your relatives and friends seem to be coping better than you are. Once again, you are wondering if there is something wrong with you, or whether you are a bad griever. Here are some questions to honestly ask yourself about how you are feeling:

- Do you avoid people, places, and things that remind you of your husband or his death?
- Do you find you still cannot admit his death happened?
- Do you feel emotionally numb?
- Are you often disconnected from everything and everyone around you?
- Do you walk around in a daze?
- Do you feel like your life has no meaning?
- Do you have trouble imagining a happy life without your husband?
- Do you feel like a part of you died with him?
- Do you no longer trust the world?
- Are you bitter and angry over his death?
- Do your feelings affect your ability to work or be a good mother?
- Do you have nightmares about your husband's death?
- Do you sometimes feel you are reliving especially painful memories?
- Are you preoccupied with his death?

- Do you anticipate other bad things happening?
- Do you get anxious or upset around the anniversary of his death or other dates that were significant to you and your husband?

If you answered "yes" to many of these questions, you may be experiencing traumatic grief or posttraumatic stress reactions related to your husband's death. The concept of traumatic grief is relatively new. According to Shear, Zuckoff, and Frank (2001), it refers to intense grief reactions that include, but are not limited to:

- being unable to accept that your husband died,
- an obsession with the details of his death,
- powerful feelings of yearning and longing for him,
- an overpowering sense of emptiness,
- a profound sense of loneliness, and
- the inability to imagine yourself feeling happy and alive again.

Posttraumatic stress reactions (Schiraldi, 2000) are, in many ways, similar to the feelings associated with traumatic grief. We have opted not to include the difference between the two; it is a distinction that matters most to health-care professionals. What matters to you is that your feelings are probably quite intense and may interfere with your ability to cope with normal, day-to-day activities.

Your feelings are shared by many military widows. These emotions are common after losing someone in a sudden and traumatic way. Knowing they are common, however, may not be enough to help you feel better.

A lot of grief work is done by talking out your feelings. This is where a structured grief workshop or a good counselor or therapist can help you feel better. Don't be reluctant to ask for help. The sudden death of your husband is usually not something you can work through alone.

YOUR GRIEF IS STIRRED UP REPEATEDLY BY PUBLICITY

In instances where your husband's death was a public event, such as the terrorist attack on USS *Cole*, or the war on terror, it may be a news item for many months or years. Sometimes you can't read a newspaper or watch television without the circumstances in which your husband was killed being replayed or rehashed ad nauseum. If you are continually upset by the ongoing publicity, here are some questions to think over:

- Do news stories related to your husband's death catch you off guard and sometimes cause you to relive the horror of the event?
- Does the release of new information about his death cause you significant distress?
- Do you feel anxious because of continuous speculation about the event in the media?
- Do you have intense reactions when comparisons are made between your husband's death and similar deaths?
- Do you feel at the mercy of the media when it comes to reporting other military deaths?
- Do new terrorist attacks produce profound feelings of dread in you?
- Does news of ongoing hostilities repeatedly churn up your feelings of loss?

If your husband died in a sudden and traumatic way, you may have experienced an obsessive need to learn every last detail about it. You likely replayed his last moments again and again in your head. This need for knowledge is not only a common reaction, but it is also very therapeutic and important to your healing. At some point, this obsession with the details of your husband's death will become less powerful and all consuming.

When the circumstances in which your husband was killed are a national or world event, however, you are subjected to continual reminders of it through investigations, congressional hearings, and media analyses and reports. Sometimes it is difficult to get through a week without seeing the event in the news. This continuous exposure can be hard on you. The circumstances that caused your husband's death are much more than a news story.

It is extraordinarily difficult to grieve your loss and move forward when the reported causes and circumstances that led to your husband's death keep changing. Because it is extremely important for you to know the details of your husband's last moments, you can become very upset to find out new and differing information weeks, months, or even years later. This is especially true when the new information sheds a different light on how and why your husband died.

You may experience intense feelings of grief with the release of this new information, almost as though you were transported back to the time when he died. You are not going crazy. Widows often find this additional or differing information very disturbing. You may feel you are re-grieving what might be a new ending to your husband's life. This is a difficult issue, and a professional counselor can help you sort it out.

YOU HAD SECONDARY LOSSES

When your husband died, you were immediately confronted with his loss. Perhaps you weren't aware there are hosts of secondary losses that can accompany his death. This list of secondary losses can be staggering. These losses may be large or small, and it will seem as though more things have been taken away from you. Once again, you have no control over your life.

Secondary losses are real and, like other losses, must be mourned. This may be a new thought for you. Don't feel overwhelmed; you grieve some of them when you grieve for your husband. Many are the result of his death. It is important to recognize these losses, though, and to understand that they are legitimate. They can be troublesome or distressing and take time to work through and resolve.

Below is a list of some of the obvious, and not so obvious, losses that young military widows may face. While some secondary losses can be predicted, others cannot be foreseen until they jump out at you, often catching you off guard.

- Place in the military community—you are no longer a part of a command or unit.
- Current home—you must move if you are living on base or post, or need to relocate from a duty station.
- Planned children—you have no chance of having any or more children with your husband.
- Standard of living—your financial status may change, depending on your husband's rate or rank.
- Promise of a predictable future—your dreams of a life with your husband are taken away.
- Married identity—you are no longer part of a couple.
- Relationships with close friends and neighbors—your closest relationships are strained.
- Contact with stepchildren—you may be denied contact by their mother.

- Sense of safety—you are robbed of feelings of protection and security.
- The ideal relationship that wasn't—you have no chance to repair a troubled marriage.

Do not underestimate how much power a secondary loss can have over you. With each of these losses, a change occurs in your life, and usually something is taken away from or denied you. You need to work through the pain of these losses as part of your grief work. Counseling can help you to do this.

YOU ARE AVOIDING YOUR GRIEF

There is no good way around grief, although you may be tempted to avoid it. Grief expert Alan Wolfelt (1993, 2003) talked about some signs that might indicate you are attempting to avoid your grief. Ask yourself these questions:

- Do you try to avoid the grief process, hoping it will get easier or go away on its own?
- Do you use food, alcohol, drugs, or sex to blunt the pain you're feeling?
- Do you jump into new relationships before you're ready for them?
- Do you "shop 'til you drop" and spend money needlessly, hoping it will make you feel better?
- Do you keep so busy with work or volunteer activities that you don't have time to feel, much less deal with your loss?
- Do you act as though your husband's death has not affected you very much?
- Have you thrown yourself into some good cause that, while important, may keep you from focusing on your own grief work?
- Do you find you're not as concerned with your grief as you are with new physical health problems you're having?

If you answered "yes" to any of these questions, you may be spending a lot of time and energy avoiding your grief. Remember, though, that when it comes to grief, it's "pay now, or pay later." It is much better to deal with your grief now. If you are avoiding your grief or trying to substitute some unhealthy behaviors, counseling can help you to get back on track. Remember that grief work, while painful in the present, will help you open up some emotional space in your life and let you live more fully in the future.

YOU ARE DEPRESSED

It is natural to feel sad and depressed after losing your husband. The average person, however, usually cannot distinguish between feelings of sadness related to grief and truly being depressed. You may not know whether or not you are depressed, or how to get out of your depression. If you feel you may be depressed, ask yourself these questions, or ask someone close to you if they see these changes in you:

- Do you feel sad or tearful every day?
- Do you find you have lost interest in most of the things you do during the day?
- Do you find you have lost or gained weight, or have you noticed a change in your appetite?
- Do you have trouble falling asleep or staying asleep all night?
- Do you feel worthless or guilty?
- Do you have problems concentrating or making decisions?
- Do you think about your death or have frequent thoughts of ending it all?
- Do you think about harming others?

If you see yourself in these questions, working with a counselor can help you to make the distinction between grief and depression. This work will get you some of the relief you crave. If you are thinking about harming yourself, your kids, or anyone else, get professional help immediately. Don't delay!

YOU ARE HAUNTED BY UNRESOLVED ISSUES

New losses often bring back memories of old losses and the feelings of sadness and heartache connected with them. Likewise, if your husband died in a traumatic way, his death may bring back other traumatic events that occurred in your life. These may include the divorce of your parents, the deaths of people close to you, relationships that ended suddenly or badly, domestic abuse, or emotional, physical, or sexual abuse you experienced as a child or an adult. When these old issues are stirred up, you may feel a strong need to talk about them again, even if you haven't thought about them in years. Counseling can help you deal with these old wounds, as well as your new loss.

HOW DO YOU FIND A THERAPIST?

The most common way to find professional help—although it may not be the best way—is to ask a friend or family member for the name of a therapist they have seen and liked. You can also contact the family services center on base or post; the Department of Veterans Affairs (VA); your pastor, rabbi, or spiritual leader; or your family doctor. In appendix B at the back of this book, we have included several professional mental health organizations that keep a database of their members. They can help you to identify a suitable therapist near you.

It would be helpful to find a therapist who is experienced with grief, loss, and trauma, and who understands the unique culture of the military. Bring this book with you and ask the therapist about his or her experience working with young widows—especially military widows. If you are not comfortable with the therapist's answers, ask for a referral to another therapist who may be better suited to help you. The therapist will not be offended if you ask for a referral.

When you first meet with a therapist, you may not know what to say. This is natural, and an experienced therapist will guide you through the initial sessions. However, if you feel you are not connecting with the therapist, or are having trouble communicating with him or her, please bring this subject up. You will be working with your therapist for a while, and you want your relationship to be mutually open and comfortable.

Once you find a therapist whom you trust and feel comfortable with, you'll work together to decide what you need and what counseling can do for you. Your therapist will help you to identify your strengths and vulnerabilities. A good therapist can also aid you in developing some new coping skills as you work through your grief and learn to live happily in a world without your husband.

The therapist you choose will assist you through your grief work, encouraging you to tell your story and to talk about your husband. He or she will listen to you long after the world has grown impatient with you and moved on. Your therapist can recognize when you are stuck on an issue, and will make suggestions to help you to resolve it. It is difficult to predict how many sessions you will need. When you realize that counseling is helping you to feel better, however, you'll look forward to your sessions.

Some counseling is offered free of charge, such as at the base or post facilities. Grief counseling is offered through the VA at no charge to family members. TRICARE also covers most, if not all, of the cost of counseling services. If your husband was killed in a violent crime, you may also be eligible for counseling through your state's crime victims compensation fund (see appendix B).

If you have never been to a therapist before, your decision to seek counseling may produce some initial anxiety. It is a choice we urge you to make, however, because we are confident you will benefit from working with a good therapist. Your mental health and welfare are of utmost importance at this fragile time in your life.

SUPPORT GROUPS

Although they are not as good at addressing personal issues as individual counseling, grief support groups can also be helpful. Hearing others discuss their losses, and the feelings associated with them, can go very far in helping you to understand that you are not alone in your grief. You may learn that your reactions are common and even predictable. In relating your story, you may find that someone in your group has had a similar experience and can share his or her coping tips.

Grief support groups are usually open-ended, meaning you can join at any time. The subject discussed on any given evening is usually picked by the members. Often the topic is an issue of concern to a group member. You can stay with the support group as long as you like; there is no set number of sessions. Members are asked to maintain the confidentiality of what they hear in the support group to protect the feelings of all. Support group leaders do not require that you talk to participate. You may choose to attend several sessions before you speak up.

WORKSHOPS

Grief workshops are different from support groups. The workshop is more structured than a support group, focusing on providing knowledge and suggesting tasks to help you to work through your grief. A workshop is offered for a set number of sessions, usually six to ten. Once a workshop begins, no new members are added. Grief workshops are offered by a variety of organizations, such as churches, hospitals, mental health facilities, and nonprofit organizations. They are beneficial because they give you tools to help you do the work of grief.

ONLINE RESOURCES

The Internet is an outlet for grief resources, including books, articles, bulletin boards, and chat rooms. Some Web sites are geared specifically to younger widows, and a few have sections on military loss. You have to check out a site to see if it has what you're looking for. If it doesn't, perhaps the site has a link to another one that may better meet your needs. Start by checking out the resources listed below. (Appendix B lists more information about these organizations, including Web addresses and contact information.)

- Gold Star Wives was founded during World War II and provides support and information to military widows. Its Web site provides information on membership, grief resources, and legislation affecting military widows and their families.
- Military One Source supplies information on a wide variety of topics on life in the military. Its Web site also includes information on grief, loss, and trauma.
- Society of Military Widows provides a checklist on its Web site for new widows and information about legislation affecting military widows.
- Tragedy Assistance Program for Survivors (TAPS) gives assistance, support, and referrals to those who have lost a loved one in military service. Its Web site furnishes information on coping with traumatic grief and making use of its online chat room. TAPS sponsors an annual "Good Grief Camp" for children whose parent died while in the military.
- U.S. Department of Veterans Affairs (VA) offers counseling for family members who have experienced a military death. Its Web site explains how to contact the VA and take advantage of its services.
- United Warrior Survivor Foundation (UWSF) provides emotional and peer support to the widows of special operations personnel. The Web site provides information on its services and programs, as well as contact information.

★   ★   ★
Lesson Learned
The more you know about military grief,
the more you understand that you are not going crazy.

Putting It All Together

The grief and trauma you are going through after losing your husband is unlike any other loss. We have talked about some of the many ways in which military grief can wreak havoc in your life. We urge you to find a counselor you can trust and with whom you are comfortable to help you through the emotional upheaval you know all too well. We cannot state strongly enough that, if you are having thoughts of harming yourself or others, call for help right now—this very moment. There is help for you. You are not alone.

CHAPTER 11

★ ★ ★

THOUGHTS OF SUICIDE

Mike and Rachael

After an abusive marriage and an ugly divorce, Rachael was a bit cynical about love in general and men in particular. Little did she know when she met that barrel-chested Marine at a friend's wedding that she would find the great love of her life. The Marine, better known as Mike, was on leave in Iowa, visiting his ten-year-old son who lived in Ames with his ex-wife.

For Mike and Rachael, the attraction was instantaneous. From the moment they met, they were inseparable. When Mike's leave was over and he returned to Camp Lejeune in North Carolina, they kept in constant contact via e-mail, instant messaging, and cell phones. Mike and Rachael were married the following New Year's Eve in a simple ceremony in front of the fireplace at her father's home. Rachael started the new year as a Marine wife, and in the middle of winter, she relocated to Camp Lejeune.

Rachael found out she was pregnant just a few days after their first wedding anniversary, and she and Mike were elated. Sometimes when Mike was away on training exercises, Rachael would stare at her reflection in a mirror and pinch her left arm, just to make sure she was awake. Her life with Mike was her dream come true.

When the grim-faced Marines arrived at her door on an unseasonably warm March day, Rachael didn't know why they were there. It was their duty to inform her that Mike was killed in a training accident. A staff sergeant in an assault amphibian battalion, he had drowned while trying to save a sinking Amtrac during a training exercise.

Rachael refused to believe that Mike was dead. It was only when she saw his body a few days later that she began to realize her idyllic life had turned into a nightmare. Tragically, Rachael miscarried Mike's baby the day after his funeral.

Mike's death and the loss of her baby sent Rachael spiraling downward. She was obsessed with the unfairness of life and wondered why her no-good ex-husband was still alive and her beloved Mike had died an early death.

As the days and nights all blended into one, Rachael began to feel she had nothing to live for. She couldn't keep the thoughts of suicide out of her head. Alone and afraid of these thoughts, she asked her CACO for help. He got her an emergency appointment at the base hospital. For the first time since Mike's death, she felt safe.

*W*E ARE NOT AFRAID TO TALK ABOUT thoughts of dying, and we hope you are not either. Widows are often reluctant to talk about this scary subject; they are ashamed of their thoughts. But there is nothing to be ashamed or embarrassed about. Our experience with grief groups has taught us that whenever you put widows together, and they are comfortable enough to talk openly and honestly, they bring up the subject of not wanting to live.

Widows have all kinds of thoughts about death. Perhaps you can identify with those who say they don't care if they live or die. While you might never think of intentionally killing yourself, maybe you have felt you would not care if you stopped breathing or were run over by the garbage truck. You may even have prayed that God would put you out of your misery. We have also seen widows engage in reckless behaviors and take unnecessary risks, hoping that something dreadful would happen to them.

We understand that, at times, you feel so badly that you don't want to live, but dying is not the answer. If you see yourself in this position, then now is the time to talk through these potentially alarming thoughts or behaviors with a professional.

There is a big difference between not wanting to live and thinking about ways to die. It is always alarming when widows think about taking their own lives. If you are having thoughts of suicide, you need to get help to understand that while these feelings and thoughts may be strong at the moment, they are always illogical and misguided. In times of hopelessness, the world can look bleak, but these feelings and thoughts will not last forever. Trust us.

★ ★ ★

Lesson Learned
Experience has taught us that life can and will improve.

You have other options, but you probably cannot see them through the fog and friction of your emotions. We don't want to minimize how awful you may be feeling, but there is no getting around the fact that suicide is a final, permanent, and drastic action. There is no second chance. We cannot stress enough that you should take these thoughts seriously and seek help.

WARNING SIGNS

Thoughts of dying are always something to be concerned about, and we urge you to take them seriously. We want to make sure you stay in an emotionally and physically safe place. Here are some questions derived from the National Mental Health Association Web site for you to consider. "Yes" answers can be red flags, indicating risky thoughts or behaviors. Take them seriously, and talk with a professional.

- Do you feel like you have no reason to go on without your husband?
- Do you engage in impulsive or high-risk behaviors, hoping that something bad will happen to you?
- Do you often say things like, "I might not be around," or "The kids will be better off without me"?
- Do you save prescribed medications "just in case" the emotional pain gets too bad?
- Do you sometimes plan who will take care of your kids and pets if you are not around?
- Are you giving away your favorite or prized possessions?
- Have you lost hope that you will ever feel better?
- Do you have a history of depression, mania, or schizophrenia?
- Have you attempted suicide in the past?

- Do you have a family history of suicide?
- Do you actively think about how you would commit suicide?
- Do you have a plan and intend to carry it out?
- Do you have the means to carry out a suicide plan?

★ ★ ★

Echo
"I honestly felt my husband wouldn't want me to die, too."

WHAT TO DO IF YOU ARE HAVING THESE THOUGHTS

Don't be caught up in thinking your feelings of pain, sorrow, isolation, or helplessness will rule the rest of your life. You have what it takes to get through this rough time. You are a survivor. As you have learned, it's a sign of sanity to reach out for help during the times you need it. If you are thinking about killing yourself, this is one of those times. If you have children, you don't want to make them orphans.

We hope you aren't trying to deal with these extreme feelings alone. Suicide is a frightening subject, but it must be met head-on. It cannot be overlooked or downplayed. If you are in counseling, talk with your therapist today about your feelings. If you don't have a counselor and you're having thoughts of suicide, get help immediately by calling your local crisis or suicide hot line. If you cannot locate a hot line in your area, dial 800-273-TALK (8255), which is a national suicide hot line. If necessary, dial 911 for assistance.

★ ★ ★

Lesson Learned
Most people who got help later said
they were glad they didn't act on their suicidal impulses.

PUTTING IT ALL TOGETHER

If you are feeling hopeless and overwhelmed by your husband's death, remember that although it is natural to be sad and depressed, suicidal thoughts should always be taken seriously. You are not alone. There are professionals waiting to help you. Make that call today.

Web sites that provide more information on suicide and how to get help are listed in appendix B at the end of this book.

CHAPTER 12

★ ★ ★

DEPLOYMENT-DELAYED GRIEF

Kevin and Mandy

Kevin and Mandy were your typical military family. In their late twenties, they had two children—a son and a young daughter—and two pets—a dog and a cat. Although he loved being a Marine, Kevin was unsure if he would stay in for twenty years; his son had ADHD, and Mandy couldn't handle him when Kevin was away. Kevin's fate as a Marine rested on how well Mandy and the kids survived the up-and-coming deployment.

Kevin had just left on a six-month cruise as part of a MEU (Marine Expeditionary Unit) on board one of the Navy's amphibious assault ships. As an air crewman, he rode in the back of a CH46-E helicopter. While attempting to land on the boat, the helo lost one of its engines, bounced off the landing pad, and rolled into the Pacific.

Kevin did not survive the mishap. It was believed he was trapped by the dislodged cargo in the cabin when the helo rolled over. His body was never recovered, but his helmet was found in the floating debris. It was kept for the JAG (Judge Advocate General) investigation and later destroyed.

Back home, with no body to bury or tangible proof of Kevin's death, it was easier for Mandy to believe he was still alive than to acknowledge that Kevin was dead. She was sure the Marine Corps had made a mistake, and Kevin would come home in six months at the end of the deployment.

Although in her heart she denied Kevin's death, Mandy cooperated with her CACO and obediently signed all the paperwork. She learned a long time ago not to buck the system. Kevin would straighten it all out when he got home.

Her denial of Kevin's death reached a point where it became a concern to her family and friends. Mandy still spoke of Kevin in the present tense, bought Christmas presents for him, and made plans for his homecoming. She refused to discuss moving out of quarters because Kevin wouldn't know where to find her when he returned.

The reality of Kevin's death finally sank in when the MEU returned without him. Six months after his death, Mandy finally began to grieve for Kevin.

ONE OF THE MAJOR DIFFERENCES between the military and civilian worlds is the concept of deployments. We know of few professions in the civilian workforce where your husband is away from home, potentially in harm's way, for weeks, months, and occasionally a year at a time. Deployments are a necessary part of the military's job to protect and defend America. They occur for peacekeeping purposes, armed combat, deterrence, humanitarian needs, and to pre-position our military assets in the world's hot spots. They are never easy, neither on the forward-deployed forces nor on the families back home. Deployments are tough enough to contend with when your husband is alive, but they take on a completely new dimension when your husband dies or is killed on deployment.

HE DIED ON DEPLOYMENT

It was especially traumatic for you when your CACO or Casualty Notification Officer brought you the life-wrecking news on what started out as an otherwise normal day. Even though you missed your husband when he was deployed, after a few weeks, you got into the routine of having him away. For the length of his deployment, it was normal that he was gone. When he died, you didn't immediately grasp the fact that he was never coming home.

Because you were far away from your husband when he died, you couldn't go to the place where it happened and see for yourself. All you had was the official death notification by military personnel; for you there was no tangible proof of your husband's death.

The shocking news, combined with the lack of physical proof and his absence because of the deployment, may propel you into a state of denial. This denial, which sometimes lasts for months, can delay your grief response if you are not careful.

Although military widows are sometimes reluctant to admit it, for a long time after you were notified, and even after the funeral and memorial services, you still believed, in your heart of hearts, that your husband was coming home. This is common among military widows. We will explain what keeps some widows in a state of denial, no matter how illogical it is.

- Your husband was *supposed* to be away. He was deployed, and, whether he was scheduled to come home in ten days or ten months, he was not scheduled to be home when he died. You probably didn't like being alone, but you adapted to a day-to-day routine that did not include him. Dead or alive, he was not physically present in your everyday life. Your husband did not take out the garbage, leave his uniform on the doorknob, or come home at the end of the day smelling like diesel fuel or hydraulic fluid.

- All the men in your husband's unit were deployed, too. You blended in with the rest of the military wives and did not stand out as the only woman without a husband. It was normal to go out just with women; they were the only ones left in town. You fit in easier when you pretended that your husband was still deployed with the others.

- You had no tangible proof of your husband's death. In all likelihood, the CACO or Casualty Notification Officer was not on scene where your husband died. Although you got this news officially from your husband's service branch, you got it second-hand—not from someone who was there. Back home, you had nothing real to see, touch, or hold that proved your husband was dead. You had no body, no pieces of wreckage, no scraps of clothing, no mangled wedding ring or dog tags. You had nothing that was with your husband when he died.

- Your husband's remains came home in a closed casket. You may have been advised not to view your husband's remains. However, when you cannot see his body, or touch his arm or leg or even a bone fragment, it's hard to believe your husband is dead. For some widows, especially Navy and Marine widows whose husbands were lost at sea, there are no remains to bury, making it even harder to accept the reality of his death.

- You continued to receive "signs of life" from him. Because the mail service from deployed units takes time, your husband's letters continued to arrive even after he died. If you were not convinced he was dead, seeing his handwriting on the envelope and reading his words may make you question whether he is truly gone. Some guys prearrange to have flowers delivered while they are deployed or on cruise. If your husband did this, it was bittersweet, and getting flowers from him after he was declared dead probably contributed to your continued denial.

- Your husband loved you too much to die on you. He was so tough and strong, and you both thought he was invincible. When he left on deployment, he promised he would take care of himself. As his wife, you knew your husband would keep that promise, find a way to survive, and come back home to you.

★　★　★

Echo

"Even though they told me my husband's body
was in that closed casket, I knew he was still alive
and on a secret mission—
and that's why he hasn't been calling or e-mailing me."

WHEN THE DEPLOYMENT ENDS

A moment of truth occurred for you when your husband's unit came home without him. Up to that point, you may have held on to a kernel of hope that your husband's death was a mistake, and he would be coming home with the returning troops. It was a harsh lesson in reality when your husband did not come home with his unit.

Some widows go to the unit's homecoming for reasons they cannot admit to or explain. They needed to be there, *just in case*. In fact, they *had* to be there, for it extinguished that small, flickering flame of hope they carried within them.

Once your husband's command came home without him, you most likely noticed your grief reactions changed, becoming more intense and painful. Some military widows feel they only started to grieve for their husbands when their units returned home without them.

With your husband's command back home, your immediate world changed again. People treated you differently. Perhaps the other military wives were less available, now that they had their husbands back home. You had the expectation that once your husband's command returned, you would be able to talk with the men who served with him. However, you found his fellow warriors were reluctant to talk with you about your husband, or worse, they shied away. With happy couples springing up like dandelions in your front yard, you became very aware that you are now alone.

IF HE WAS NOT DEPLOYED WHEN HE DIED

Deployments can affect your grief even if your husband was not deployed when he died. If your husband was in a service branch that deployed regularly, over the years you developed successful coping skills to survive his deployments. These same coping skills most likely kicked in when your husband died. Because a good military wife can handle anything during a deployment, you may have held up very well—whatever that means—after your husband's death. Your internal alarm clock rang around the time your husband's deployment usually ended, signaling to you that it was time for him to come home. When he not only didn't come home but also remained dead, you may have fallen apart, experiencing some intense grief reactions, possibly for the first time since he died.

★ ★ ★

Lesson Learned

*If you aren't careful, deployment-delayed grief
can get in the way of successfully working through your loss.*

PUTTING IT ALL TOGETHER

You have a greater risk of denying your husband's death if it occurred while he was on deployment, or if he deployed regularly. Denial isn't always a bad thing because it allows you to accept in small, tolerable doses the fact that he is not coming back. Continued denial of your husband's death, however, is unhealthy.

Deployments are another element that complicate military grief. Grief support and counseling can help you navigate these complexities of military loss.

CHAPTER 13

★ ★ ★

DISENFRANCHISED GRIEF

Dan and Abbey

Dan and Abbey were good friends in the kayaking club in college before they fell in love and married. Now, two years and one child later, they still loved kayaking but learned that babies take up lots of time and energy.

Dan, a first lieutenant in the Air Force, had just returned home from a deployment in Qatar. While walking out of the base gym, he ran into a buddy from Qatar, and they headed off to a local watering hole to swap war stories and catch up. A couple of laughs and a few beers later, he headed home to his wife and child.

Driving into the setting sun, Dan couldn't see the red light. He drove through an intersection, hitting a gray sedan and propelling both vehicles into the path of an oncoming truck. The family in the sedan was killed instantly. Dan, who wasn't wearing a seat belt, was thrown out of his SUV and died before the police arrived on scene.

While cooking dinner, Abbey had the television on for background noise. Her ears perked up when she heard of a fatal accident at a major intersection near their house. Abbey figured that was why Dan wasn't home yet. Little did she know he would never come home again.

The accident left the town shocked and they rallied around both families. When it was reported that Dan's blood alcohol level exceeded the legal limit, however, it became apparent that Dan was the cause of the accident. This news spread through the town like wildfire.

People Abbey thought were friends stayed away. Those few who did stop by mumbled some awkward condolences and left quickly. Abbey didn't know what to say in reply. She felt more alone than ever and believed she was paying the price for Dan's actions.

Abbey moved far away from the town where they lived. She was still deeply troubled over losing Dan and his role in causing the deaths of a family of four. Abbey knew Dan was a good guy who would never intentionally hurt anyone. She realized she couldn't work through these issues on her own and sought counseling.

SOME MILITARY WIDOWS FEEL THEIR GRIEF is minimized, downplayed, or outright ignored by other people. Noted grief educator Kenneth Doka (2002) has written that there are certain circumstances under which a person's right to grieve may be disenfranchised. This means his or her grief is not fully recognized, acknowledged, or supported by others—even close friends and family members.

HOW YOUR GRIEF MAY BE DISENFRANCHISED BY OTHERS

YOUR LOSS WAS NOT ALWAYS RECOGNIZED

Perhaps you weren't married yet but had a long-standing romantic relationship with someone who died in the military. You had an approaching wedding date but your fiancé died before the wedding took place. You weren't considered the primary next of kin, even though you were the love of his life.

Because the military must abide by the law, your place in his heart could not be reflected in your status as a legal survivor. In these situations, you had no legal rights or benefits as a surviving spouse, such as receiving financial compensation or helping to plan the funeral. If you were excluded from funeral planning, which is important in helping you to accept the reality of his death, you may have felt your loss wasn't adequately recognized or respected. If so, this may have sparked feelings of anger or resentment within you.

YOUR LOSS WAS NOT ALWAYS ACKNOWLEDGED

Some people may not realize or acknowledge the extent of your loss. For example, if you and your husband were newlyweds, people may have thought your loss was minimal, because your marriage was measured in months, not decades. They were measuring your loss by time, not by the depth of your emotional connection to your husband. We know of several widows who were asked by their husband's family to return all of his personal possessions. The family members believed their long-standing relationship had priority over your marriage.

★ ★ ★

Echo

*"When we got home from the funeral,
my mother-in-law asked me to give back
all of my husband's baby and childhood pictures."*

Secondary losses, such as the loss of your military lifestyle or the potential to have children with your husband, are usually not recognized or acknowledged. Therefore, you don't get the understanding or support you need in order to deal with them.

YOU WERE NOT GIVEN THE OPPORTUNITY TO GRIEVE

Occasionally, some people act as judge and jury to those who are bereaved. Perhaps you and your husband had a troubled relationship or were in the process of getting divorced. People who knew your relationship was rocky might feel you don't need to grieve for him. If you believe that others think this way or, worse, blame you for his death, you may feel denied the right to mourn his passing, and notice that your displays of grief are treated with disdain.

YOUR HUSBAND'S DEATH WAS STIGMATIZED

Maybe your husband was responsible for his own death or the deaths of others. If so, your loss and your right to grieve may not be publicly acknowledged. Perhaps the circumstances of his death caused others to stigmatize both you and your husband; that often happens in suicide, homicide, or accidental death. When deaths of this type occur, people may blame you for your husband's actions, and their opinions may be obvious by the way they treat you. For example, they may not show support or sympathy toward you. Even though your needs are complicated by this type of death, your social support may be minimal to nonexistent.

★ ★ ★

Echo

*"When we were leaving the memorial service on post,
the mother of one of the crew members told me
that my husband killed her son, because he was the pilot."*

HOW YOU GRIEVE YOUR HUSBAND'S DEATH

Sometimes people acknowledge your husband's death and your right to grieve, but they are critical of *how* you grieve. If they decide that the way you grieve is different from how *they* would grieve, they may see your behavior as unacceptable. Perhaps someone says, "You're taking too long," or, "You should be over this by now," as though you have some choice in the matter. You may also have been told, "It's wrong to feel that way" when you express your anger with the military or God because your husband died. These statements suggest there is something wrong with you—that you have the right to grieve, but not the way you're doing it.

IF YOUR GRIEF IS DISENFRANCHISED BY OTHERS

If any of these situations sound familiar to you, your right to grieve your husband's death has probably been disenfranchised. If you continue to seek the support you need and deserve from relatives and friends who are not there for you, you will probably find yourself feeling worse. In that case, it is probably better to find emotional support outside of your usual circle of family and friends.

Look for others who can validate your feelings and provide support. Talking with a counselor or a member of the clergy may help you understand that, if your grief isn't recognized, acknowledged, or supported, it can only add to the anguish you feel.

★ ★ ★
Lesson Learned
Talk with someone who will listen to you
and validate your legitimate feelings of loss and grief.

PUTTING IT ALL TOGETHER

When your husband dies, your loss may not be recognized, acknowledged, or supported by others in a number of ways. You may feel misunderstood, frustrated, and isolated, even from family and friends. If this is your experience, remember that grief is a reaction to losing someone very dear to you. These feelings are valid.

PART FOUR

The Unplanned Trip through Living Hell

CHAPTER 14

★ ★ ★

THE MILITARY TAKES CARE OF ITS OWN

Dave and Andrea

Dave was a forty-eight-year-old colonel in the Army Corps of Engineers. He and Andrea had been married for twenty-five years and had four children: twin sons and two younger daughters. With both daughters soon to graduate from college, Dave and Andrea were looking forward to having the house to themselves.

Always the engineer, Dave was making plans to start a consulting business, which he would run from their home when he retired. Andrea, who was often Mom and Dad to their kids when Dave was away, was thrilled at the prospect of having Dave home on a permanent basis.

Dave and Andrea had strong ties to the military: both were Army brats. Dave was second-generation West Point, and Andrea's father had been a field artilleryman. Being a military dependent was the only world Andrea knew. After a lifetime of the Army way of life, however, she felt she had paid her dues. With Dave's retirement date approaching, she found herself dreaming about this new chapter in their lives.

One Friday morning, Andrea was sitting in her sunroom, checking out some interior design courses at the local college, when the doorbell rang. She was expecting her good friend, Deanna. Instead, a Casualty Notification Officer informed her that Dave had had an aneurysm at his desk. He died before the paramedics could get him to the hospital.

Dave's sudden death was a staggering blow to Andrea on many levels. Andrea's casualty officer explained her benefits and entitlements as Dave's widow, but he could not tell her where she now fit within the Army infrastructure.

The only life Andrea had ever known was as an Army dependent: first as an Army brat and later as an officer's wife. In addition to losing Dave, Andrea realized she lost her military lifestyle. She was no longer an Army wife or part of a unit, but she wasn't a civilian either.

As a military widow, Andrea didn't know where she fit in. For the first time in her life, she realized there was no place for her in the Army.

*Y*OU HAVE DUTIFULLY SIGNED AND DATED every paper your casualty officer placed before you. You have neatly stacked on your dining room table all the pamphlets, folders, and booklets you were given. But even with all this information, you have stared at your new ID card and wondered, "Am I still a dependent?"

Like other military widows, you may be concerned about whether you and your children are still military dependents and eligible for the benefits and services that were available to you when your husband was alive. The simple answer is that you are still a dependent, but your status has changed from that of a spouse to one of a URW (un-remarried widow), and some of your benefits changed along with it.

BENEFITS AND ENTITLEMENTS

Benefits for military widows are provided by the DoD (Department of Defense), the VA, and the Social Security Administration. Some states also offer benefits, entitlements, grants, and tax breaks to the families of deceased service members, especially members of the National Guard.

We are not experts on benefits and do not want to pass on inaccurate or changing information on such an important topic. Your best resource for current and accurate benefit information is your casualty officer. If you cannot get the information you need from your casualty officer, we suggest you use the chain of command in the casualty section of your husband's service branch. Talk with the local or regional casualty representative. If you still don't find the answers you are looking for, we have included in appendix B contact information so you can reach the person in charge of the casualty assistance office for your service branch. This appendix also includes Web sites that will explain how your TRI-CARE medical and dental benefits change when your husband dies.

THE MILITARY TAKES CARE OF ITS OWN?

For as long as you were a military spouse, you believed that the military took care of its own. This was true on many different levels at every duty station. For example, there were spouses clubs, deployment support groups, and numerous other social and support groups that were specific to military life. They provided emotional support and practical suggestions on how to survive and enjoy a duty station. Classes were offered on everything from balancing your checkbook to relocating outside CONUS (continental United States).

When your husband died, you automatically assumed that the military would take care of you and your children, as they did when he was alive. When this didn't happen in the ways you expected, you likely felt hurt and abandoned, by either your husband's command or his service branch. Like many military widows, you expected more from the military establishment and the people with whom your husband served.

The problem is that the military and the widow have different views of what "taking care of the widow" means. It is in the gap created by these differing views that the widow often feels cast aside. We will try to explain why this gap occurs.

From the military's perspective, casualty assistance was immediately provided to you as a new widow. As we explained in chapter 5, this assistance came in the form of a casualty officer who helped with your immediate needs, assisted you with your husband's funeral or memorial service, and took you through the bureaucratic maze of forms, documents, and red tape following your husband's death.

As a new military widow, you *expected* the military to take care of these details, and it did. You also *expected* the military to help you with the emotional wreckage that was created by your husband's death, for as long as it took you to get back on your feet again. After all, you and your husband were part of the military family, and as you were told many times, the military takes care of its own.

Your husband's command probably rallied around you after he died and offered you and your family continuous support up to and through the funeral and memorial service. The phone calls and visits probably tapered off as the weeks rolled past, and by the three-month mark, they were few and far between. In all likelihood, you found this bewildering, disturbing, or upsetting. You thought, of all people and organizations, your husband's command would be there to offer ongoing emotional support, just as they did immediately after his death.

Perhaps you expected that your husband's command would still regard you as a wife, and you would be treated like the other spouses. As often happens with military widows, you probably assumed you would still be invited to all unit functions, such as change of command, promotion, and retirement ceremonies. You also expected to be included in such other command functions as holiday parties, deployment homecomings, hail and farewells, and the military birthday balls. If—and most likely, when—you were not invited to these functions, you probably felt some unexpected losses: that of your place within the military community and, possibly, your military support system or social structure.

A few military widows find it too painful to stay connected to their husband's unit, so they pull away from the command and the military rather quickly. If you are one of these women, the diminished contact on the part of your husband's unit was probably not a problem for you. If you are one of the many widows for whom the military was a way of life, however, you expected continued contact from your husband's command and service branch. You were not prepared for the military to distance itself.

The distancing on the part of your husband's command usually happens subtly, and the realization that you are no longer a part of his command takes place in increments. Until *you* figure out that you are no longer a part of your husband's unit, you will get your feelings hurt. These reactions can range from being angry to feeling forgotten or abandoned.

The military distances itself from the widow on several levels. In the case of your husband's command, they do care about you, although they may not, or cannot, show it in the ways you need. For the unit and their spouses, you are a living reminder of your husband's death, and many cannot get past that reminder.

Although it's hard not to take it personally, you need to understand that your husband's command does not want you around, because they can't deal with you as his widow. If it happened to your husband, it can happen to one of them. In the business of war fighting, the military must focus on the mission and live in the present. On the other hand, you may have expected your husband's command to help you out, just as you know your husband would have assisted a unit widow, if the circumstances were different.

On another level, there's an unspoken expectation in the military that, after the widow has received her benefits, she will go away, much like a wounded puppy, to lick her wounds in private. There is the belief that the widow will naturally *want* to go back to her old civilian life—which isn't always the case. When the military way of life becomes a part of who you are, it is often difficult to let go. Ask any retired veteran.

The civilian sector operates under the assumption that the military provides continuous support to its own; consequently, there are few civilian resources that understand the complexities of military widowhood. Couple this with the military's belief that the widow willingly and fully returns to civilian life. This leaves the military widow without a firm footing in either world. Each world assumes the other will assist her. As a result, neither the military nor the civilian sector is adequately prepared to help the widow with the long-term emotional, psychological, physical, social, and spiritual issues created by military loss.

The war on terror—including Operation Enduring Freedom and Operation Iraqi Freedom—highlighted this disconnect between the military and civilian communities when it comes to the ongoing care of the military widow and her family. The government enacted legislation and set up programs to help her on a long-term basis. This is a good start toward helping the military widow, and these measures will, we hope, produce the changes needed to begin to bridge the chasm between the military and civilian sectors. Likewise, the civilian community must recognize they have a vital role in helping all military widows, especially those who live far from military facilities and installations.

One military community that does appear to look after its widows is the Special Operations community. Their approach offers some good lessons learned that are applicable to all service branches for the long-term support of and assistance to widows and children of fallen warriors.

★   ★   ★

Lesson Learned
Military widows remain dependents,
but they are no longer military spouses.

PUTTING IT ALL TOGETHER

Even though you remain a military dependent, your status within the military has changed. You are a dependent without a living sponsor. You are no longer affiliated with a particular command or unit.

It is difficult to figure out where you fit in, or if you fit in at all. The change in your status from military wife to widow has probably been fraught with great potential to have your feelings hurt.

The unspoken lack of acceptance of, or comfort with, military widows within the military infrastructure is a key aspect of what contributes to making military grief complex.

CHAPTER 15

★ ★ ★

DEALING WITH THE KIDS

Johnny and Gina

Johnny and Gina had been married just over ten years, and it definitely wasn't a marriage made in heaven. Johnny had a tendency to drink too much, and when he was drinking, he got ugly. Each time, it was the same old story. Johnny was sweet and apologetic the next day, swearing he would change. Gina always believed him, but as the years rolled past, she found she liked it better when Johnny had sea duty. Then, Gina and their daughter, Tiffany, lived an uneventful and quiet life. Gina thought about getting a divorce, but she didn't know how she would make it on her own, so she stayed with Johnny.

Johnny was an E6 in the Navy and stationed on an aircraft carrier, which was homeported in Norfolk, Virginia. On board the ship he was an aviation ordnanceman, or a "red shirt," to use the language of the flight deck. When Johnny left on a six-month deployment in the middle of November, Gina decided to take Tiffany to Boston to spend Christmas with her family. It was the first time Tiffany had ever had a white Christmas. For Gina, it brought back memories of happier times.

Three days after Christmas, while directing the storage of munitions for the day's flight operations, Johnny was blown off the flight deck and into the Mediterranean Sea. The carrier strike group conducted a thorough search, but in the end, Johnny's body was never recovered.

The Navy tracked Gina down at her parents' home in Boston, where they notified her that Johnny was lost at sea and presumed dead. Gina's initial reaction embarrassed her; she was relieved that Johnny was dead. It meant an end to living with a man whom she feared more than she loved. With no body to bury, Gina couldn't have a funeral for Johnny. For her daughter's sake, she had a small memorial service.

Once the CACO finished her responsibilities, Gina and Tiffany settled back into their quiet routine. Gina focused all her energy on ensuring that her daughter was adjusting to her father's death. When the carrier strike group came home from deployment, Gina found herself thinking constantly about Johnny. She was surprised that she missed him—not the Johnny who drank, but the Johnny she knew a long time ago. Gina felt sad that she would never see *that* Johnny again.

*A*LTHOUGH YOU MAY FEEL YOU HAVE ENOUGH on your plate, if you have children, they will need some extra help to cope with your husband's death. You have lost your spouse, with whom you shared the responsibility for these kids. Your kids have lost their father, who was the most important man in their young lives. Most likely, they are upset, confused, and scared. They look to you for comfort and the security of knowing they will not lose you as well.

Because each family size is different, and the ages of children vary, the issues you face may be different from other widows. For example, some children were not yet born when their father died, or they were too young to understand what was happening. If so, you will have to decide when and how to tell them about their father. This is the type of situation you would have probably discussed with your husband. Knowing that you can't makes his absence even more obvious.

Many widows notice more of the characteristic quirks that their children share with their father after he has died. This can be both endearing and disconcerting. It is especially poignant when children who were too young to know their father suddenly and uncannily begin to move, sound, and act like him.

How Children Deal with Death

Here are some things to consider about how children deal with death:

- Like adults, children are individuals, and they mourn their losses in different ways. However, children lack the maturity, coping skills, and fundamental understanding of life and death that many adults possess. Don't expect your kids to mourn in the same way or at the same time. For example, some children may want to spend more time alone and will isolate themselves. Others become clingy, wanting to be with you and their siblings more than before.

- Their father's death is probably your kids' first loss, and it is a major one. It will be with them for a lifetime. They will need a great deal of love and support, both now and as they grow into adulthood.

- Your husband's death has forced you into a different kind of relationship with your children. That means your children are dealing with two losses: they lost their father through death, and they lost their "old" mother.

- Children may secretly worry, "What happens if Mommy dies, too?"

- Children must deal with trauma and grief, just like you. Sudden, traumatic deaths are difficult and complicated for your children as well.

- Children also have secondary losses. These may include changing their daily routine, attending a different school, or moving away and leaving close friends.

- Young children may not understand the concept that death is permanent. They think about things in a concrete or specific way. For example, if kids are told that their father "went to sleep," they may equate sleeping with dying.

- Children are more physical than adults in expressing their feelings of grief. They may act out or escalate to out-of-control behaviors.

- Children may ask the same questions about their father over and over again. They like to hear about him.

- Children will grieve on and off over time. They may think about their father's death and be sad, then go out and play shortly afterward.

- Children grieve differently, depending upon their ages and developmental levels. They will need to revisit their father's death at each new level of growth and maturity.
- Children often try to protect you from their feelings. They may not mention their father or cry in front of you if they know it upsets you.
- Children sometimes take on adult roles after their father's death. Boys may want to become the "man of the house," for example, while girls may mother their younger siblings.
- Depending upon your family's religious beliefs, your children may wonder what happened to their father's soul or spirit.

★ ★ ★

Echo
"How long will my Daddy stay dead?"

WHAT YOU CAN DO TO HELP YOUR CHILDREN
Your children need more from you now than they did before their father died. Knowing you are solely responsible for your kids—especially now when you are likely feeling overwhelmed—can be scary for you.

Here are some suggestions for helping your children deal with their issues of grief and loss:
- Comfort them with frequent hugs and other affectionate gestures.
- Reassure your kids that they are still loved and will be cared for.
- Try to understand the loss from your child's point of view.
- Share stories of your husband with your kids. Show them pictures, videotapes, and DVDs of their dad, so he will live in their memories.
- Give them something that belonged to their father to keep in their own room. If your kids are very young, show it to them but hold onto it until they are old enough to appreciate it. Alan Wolfelt (2000) talks about creating a "memory box" for your child. This might include pictures, cards, birth announcements, and other irreplaceable items.
- Allow your child to feel what he or she feels. If your kids are old enough, give them a small stack of pictures of faces with differ-

ent expressions. Encourage them to put one on the refrigerator each day to show how they are feeling. Talk with your children about why they chose a particular picture, and what it means to them.

- Make sure your child's teacher knows about the loss, so that extra support can be provided.
- Let your children help plan ways to honor their father's life, especially around his birthday, the anniversary of his death, or Memorial Day and Veterans Day.

When Do You Get Help for Your Children?

Seeing your kids grieve is difficult and adds another layer of worry for you. Sometimes it is hard to know when their behavior indicates they are getting into trouble and could benefit from outside help. Here are some things to look for:

- Your child is acting out or showing aggressive behaviors, such as hitting other kids or throwing temper tantrums.
- Your child has regressed to behaviors that he or she had outgrown, like bed-wetting or thumb sucking.
- Your child seems to have withdrawn from others, including family and friends.
- Your child is having problems in school. For example, his or her grades have dropped, or teachers are reporting behavioral changes.
- Your kid's behavior makes you wonder whether he or she is using alcohol or drugs.
- Your child tells you he or she is having fantasies of dying and being reunited with Dad.

If you are worried about your child's behavior, speak to a counselor trained to help children who are grieving. If your child is talking about killing him- or herself or wanting to die to rejoin Dad, get help immediately. It is better to be overprotective than to risk yet another tragedy.

★ ★ ★
Lesson Learned
Kids are still kids, and they grieve in different ways.

PUTTING IT ALL TOGETHER

Grief work is not easy for anyone. Just as you should allow others to help you, do not hesitate to let others help your children through this difficult process. Your kids will probably need some help to work through their father's death. The trick is to address their mourning needs, while still encouraging them to be kids. It is important you don't go overboard trying to meet your children's needs as a way of avoiding your own grief work. Make sure you have some time away from them to tend to *you*.

Appendix B includes several Web sites that provide information that can help you to better understand what your children are going through. These sites offer age-appropriate information about grieving that targets children, teenagers, and the adults who help them. They also make available information about how to find local support groups for children in your area. Some sites list books that address the specific concerns of children after a loved one has died through either suicide or murder. Other Web sites provide information on grief camps for children.

CHAPTER 16

★ ★ ★

DUMB THINGS PEOPLE SAY

Clarence and Jasmine

Clarence and Jasmine had been married just a few months. Most of that time, Clarence was away for basic electronics training at Keesler AFB in Biloxi, Mississippi. While he was at school, Jasmine stayed in Tallahassee, where their families lived. To keep her company, Clarence gave Jasmine a puppy. She named him Shrimp, after Clarence's favorite food. Jasmine quickly fell in love with this little fur ball.

The couple were on their way to their first duty station, Offutt AFB in Nebraska. The two of them, Shrimp, and their pots and pans were packed tightly into their tiny car. The newlyweds were excited about finally starting their new life together.

As they drove toward Omaha, it abruptly got colder. With the drop in temperature came an early and unexpected snowstorm. The excitement of seeing snow for the first time quickly dissipated when the highway became slick. Clarence had little experience driving on hazardous roads. With the worsening storm approaching whiteout conditions, he never saw the jackknifed truck in front of him.

When Jasmine regained consciousness in the hospital a few days later, she found her mother keeping watch at her bedside. It broke her mother's heart to tell Jasmine that Clarence didn't survive. Jasmine then asked for Shrimp, her furry little friend. When she learned she lost both Clarence and Shrimp, Jasmine was inconsolable.

Hoping to make Jasmine feel better, one of the staff told her that she was young and pretty, and she would find another husband. She also told Jasmine she was lucky that Shrimp was only a dog, and not her baby. These statements, meant to make her feel better, only made Jasmine feel worse.

*a*S YOU HAVE DISCOVERED, people say some pretty dumb things to widows. This seems to be a universal phenomenon. What is even more baffling is that the people who blurt out these comments usually know you. They can be family, friends, or casual acquaintances.

Why Do People Say Dumb Things?

Believe it or not, they are not trying to hurt you. In fact, these folks are well intentioned, and they are trying to make you feel better. Their efforts often backfire, though, and their comments sound unsympathetic and thoughtless.

Hearing some of these comments, you may feel as though people are minimizing your loss. They don't understand it, they can't relate, and what they say sounds hollow. Or, they try to connect with you by comparing a much different loss in their lives to your husband's death. This can leave you feeling annoyed, exasperated, or hurt.

Here are a few reasons why people who are trying to comfort you might put their feet in their mouths. We hope you understand that, behind every seemingly insensitive comment, there are good intentions.

- People want you to feel better. They will often say something in the hope it will ease your pain. They are trying to fix your grief. They dislike seeing you miserable, and they think their comments will bring you consolation or comfort.
- People are at a loss for words. When people don't know what to say, they sometimes feel inadequate. Unfortunately, most people don't understand that a simple "I'm sorry for your loss" can speak volumes. People are often awkward and uncomfortable in expressing condolences. This gives them a greater need to keep talking and fix your grief.
- People are personally struggling with your husband's death. Some people will attempt to comfort you in the hope of finding

comfort themselves. They may be struggling with their own feelings about your husband's death. By making you feel better, they give themselves permission to ease some of their own discomfort. If you appear to be doing well, then they can feel better, too.

- Your husband's death brings back memories of loss for them. Some people will offer you comfort in ways that helped them, when they dealt with loss. The words of condolence that worked for them may not work for you, but they don't know it. You are left to wonder how a good friend or family member could make such a remark.
- People seek answers to death within their religious beliefs. Just as you search for a spiritual understanding of your husband's death, so do those around you. A problem arises when their religious beliefs differ from yours. It may seem as though others are imposing their beliefs on you. What may be comforting to them can be upsetting or even offensive to you.
- Your husband's death threatens some people's sense of immortality. For some of your friends—especially those who served with your husband, and their spouses—your husband's death was too close. To figure out why they lived and he died, some people will rationalize his death to protect their own feelings of vulnerability.

Dumb Things People Say

This chapter would be incomplete without a list of those priceless "words of wisdom" you have heard and endured. Because you have probably heard most of these little gems, with a healthy dose of widow humor we have also included what you at one time or another secretly wanted to say in reply.

- "You're young. You'll find another husband." (I don't want to "find" another husband. I liked the one I had. I just want him back.)
- "I know exactly how your feel. My (dog . . . cat) died last year." (Just how crazy are you? You're comparing the loss of your cat to my husband's death?)
- "It was God's will." (Oh? If you're speaking for God these days, then we need to talk!)

- "God always takes the good ones first." (So what does that say about me, now that I'm left here without him? P.S. Does God know you're speaking for him again?)
- "God doesn't give you more than you can handle." (Let me get this straight. If I were weak, my husband would still be alive and here with me? Can you double-check this one with God?)
- "It was his time to go." (While you have the departure schedule handy, can I see it?)
- "He's happy where he is." (The last time I saw him, he looked pretty happy with me and the kids.)
- "You must get on with your life." (What life? I just buried the heart and soul of my future.)
- "Don't dwell on his death. Cherish your memories." (What memories? We were married for only six months, and he was deployed for three of them.)
- "You look good." (Hmmm . . . I wonder what you would say if I looked like I feel inside?)
- "It could be worse." (That's right. I could live the next seventy years without him.)
- "I don't know how I'd survive in your shoes." (Let's switch places and you can find out!)

★   ★   ★

Lesson Learned

Too many people speak before they think.

PUTTING IT ALL TOGETHER

People say all kinds of things to widows. Some of these comments seem silly at best and completely insensitive at worst. While people say these things to make you feel better, you know that some of these comments were better left unspoken.

If you do find yourself on the receiving end of dumb comments, try not to be thrown by them. Chalk it up as another widow experience. If nothing else, you'll have a good story to share with other widows as you commiserate over a glass of wine.

CHAPTER 17

★ ★ ★

GOD ISSUES

Brad and Kirsten

Each time they were transferred, Brad and Kirsten intended to become members of a local church, but they never got around to it. After September 11, 2001, Kirsten decided it was time, and she joined the post chapel. There, she found a number of wives like herself, women who were worried about our country and the safety of their husbands who would again be going into harm's way. When Brad, a Green Beret captain, deployed to Afghanistan, Kirsten joined a weekly prayer group at the chapel.

During a HAHO (high altitude, high opening) insertion into the mountains of Afghanistan, Brad's main parachute malfunctioned. When he attempted to cut it away, the main chute became entangled on his equipment. Unable to clear it, Brad deployed his reserve parachute, which got entangled with the main chute. Out of options in the Afghan night, Brad was killed on impact.

Not emotionally ready to relocate, Kirsten stayed near Fort Bragg in North Carolina after Brad died. This was the last place she and Brad had lived together, and she felt comfortable within the Special Forces community. She also believed her prayer group at the chapel helped keep her sane.

Ten days after New Year's, Kirsten woke up with a sharp pain in her right side. It was bad, but not enough to keep her from work. By the time she got to her job, however, her condition had deteriorated, and she collapsed just a few feet from her desk.

Kirsten was taken to a nearby hospital where she nearly died from a ruptured appendix.

When she was discharged from the hospital, Kirsten was weak, both physically and spiritually. She was furious at God for letting her live. Kirsten felt that death would have put her out of her misery and reunited her with Brad.

Kirsten refused to go back to her prayer group because she and God weren't on speaking terms. In a God-sponsored coincidence, while she was at the hospital for a follow-up appointment, she ran into the chaplain who often led the prayer group. With no place to escape in the waiting room, Kirsten was forced to talk to him. Afterward, she decided to meet with the chaplain again and talk about the spiritual mess in her life.

*a*LL MILITARY WIVES KNOW their husbands' jobs can be dangerous at times. If you were like many wives, you didn't think about it too often or worry unnecessarily. In private moments, you probably asked God to protect him; most military wives pray for their husbands' safety. Few talk about those prayers, though. Because you believed that God heard your prayers and your husband would be safe, you may have had some real issues with God when the unthinkable happened, and your husband did not return home.

You probably have a personal view of God and the role he holds in your life. Up to this point, you most likely never gave much thought to the role God plays in death. We come from a Judeo-Christian background, with a defined view of life and death. But whatever your belief about God or another higher power, experience has taught us that death, especially a sudden and traumatic one, can rattle your beliefs and shake up your existing relationship with him.

In those dark days after your husband's death, you may have doubted that God listened to your prayers. Worse, you may have thought that God heard your prayers but ignored them. Maybe, like so many other military widows, you wondered why God answered other wives' prayers and brought their husbands home safely, while your prayers went unanswered.

THE UNANSWERABLE WHY'S

In trying to make sense of why your husband died, you probably went down many avenues, searching for understanding and peace of mind on a spiritual or a cosmic level. Widows are not alone on this quest. Many people facing adverse or traumatic circumstances embark on a similar search. It's natural to hunt for an understanding of why tragedy occurs. In this search for answers, you likely asked these questions of no one in particular, and everyone in general:

- Why did God take my husband from me?
- How is this God's will?
- If he is all-powerful, why didn't God save my husband?
- Why did God ignore me when I prayed for my husband's safety?
- Why did my husband die, but bad people go on living?
- Was my husband punished for something he did?
- Was I not worthy of love and a good marriage?

Looking for answers to life's tough questions is not at all unusual. In fact, people of all faiths have struggled with unanswerable questions for thousands of years.

Maybe you did more than question God. We know firsthand that widows can get mad at him. When you want to hold someone accountable for your husband's death, who better to blame than God? Perhaps, like other military widows before you, you stormed outside one moonlit night, raised your fist to the heavens, and demanded answers from God: "Why? Why him? Why me?"

While you were yelling at God, you probably didn't get the answers you were looking for. That's because, as a rule, God does not yell back. A chaplain once told us that it's okay to yell at God—at least you're talking to him. What really matters is that once you are done yelling, you keep searching for the peace of mind you seek.

Some widows don't yell at God; they stop speaking to him altogether. They give God the silent treatment, hoping he will make the first move. If you recall, the silent treatment didn't work very well when you were married. When you are not on speaking terms, you silently stew and get angrier by the moment. Nothing gets resolved unless you communicate. The same goes for your relationship with God.

WHY DO BAD THINGS HAPPEN?

There is no getting around the fact that "bad things happen to good people," to quote Rabbi Harold Kushner (1981). In fact, if you watch the news, you know that bad things happen to good people all the time. Innocent children are kidnapped, mothers are killed by drunk drivers, earthquakes level villages, and good men die young. But when bad things happen to you and those you love, it gets personal.

Over the ages, many people have asked why, if God is all-powerful and all-knowing, he allows bad things to happen to good people. He also allows bad things to happen to bad people, but generally, mankind does not see that as a problem. Likewise, God allows good things to happen to both good and bad people.

While we cannot speak for God, it appears to us that he does not micromanage the world, at least not in the ways we want him to. The reason we believe this is that he gave us the gift of free will. With this gift, we have the opportunity to make choices in our lives—choices that affect us and those around us. An aspect of free will that has troubled mankind throughout the ages is that the bad guys have this gift, too. A good example is the September 11 terrorist attacks on America.

★ ★ ★

Lesson Learned

No one is free of trials or adversity—
no person, pope, or president.

When bad things happen, we do not believe that God leaves you alone in your misery. Rather, we think God is present to support and comfort you—if you allow him into your grief. You simply need to ask for his help and be open to the ways he will provide it. His help comes in many forms, some obvious, others subtle.

Let's look at your husband's death. We believe God worked through your family, your friends, and your husband's command, starting with those first few anguished days. We believe God was present in the casseroles, the sympathy cards, the heartfelt hugs, and the people who let you cry on their shoulders. He was also there in the middle of the night when it was just you and an empty bed. God was always present. He did not abandon you.

★　★　★
Echo

*"I felt in my heart that God
grieved with me in my worst moments."*

THE SEARCH FOR ANSWERS

Ever since sorrow and loss became part of our world, men and women have pleaded with God for answers to those crucial "why" questions. Like your ancient ancestors, you would prefer God to answer them in bold ways, much like Moses carried the Ten Commandments down Mount Sinai. Today, you would probably like an e-mail from God because it's a much faster way of communicating. Just like the people of old, however, you can get frustrated when God doesn't talk to you on your terms. God does speak to you, but usually it's in quiet ways. Sometimes, you can't hear him above the racket blaring in your noisy life.

Perhaps now is the time to start talking with God again, even if you have nothing to say. Just listen with an open heart. If you give God the chance, we believe he will guide you in your search for answers.

There is great value in this spiritual search, but you have to be willing to work for it. Just like your journey through grief, you will learn more about yourself, and maybe a bit more about God, too. It does not matter how much or how little faith you have when you start—what's important is that you persevere.

We are pretty certain God won't be e-mailing you any time soon, but he has put in your life a wealth of resources in the form of men and women of faith, and countless volumes of literature on spirituality and religion. You can start by reading the Bible or other religious books of substance, praying with a fragile but willing heart, and talking to the religious leaders of your faith. Contemplate what you read and hear, and don't be afraid to ask questions or challenge what you learn.

You may never find all the answers you want. We are confident, though, that you can find a greater spiritual acceptance of your husband's death and, with that, peace of mind. You will probably get to know God better as well. Many widows have said that their faith in God was strengthened by their spiritual search after their husband's death.

★ ★ ★

Lesson Learned

*The only answers you can live with are
those you arrive at yourself.*

PUTTING IT ALL TOGETHER

We have presented our personal insights on God's role in life and death in this chapter. You may agree with us and find some comfort in our explanation. You may also disagree with our views. If so, we hope this will motivate you to seek your own personal understanding of God. Either way, we hope you continue on your own private path of figuring out not only God's role in your husband's death, but also his role in your life. You can find meaning in the rest of your life without your husband, and we feel God can help you find it.

CHAPTER 18

★ ★ ★

INAPPROPRIATE ADVANCES

Zack and Christie

Zack, a lance corporal, was stationed at the Marine Corps Air Station Miramar in California. One of Zack's buddies was heading to Iraq and needed to sell his motorcycle. Zack liked the bike and, right after payday, he became the proud owner of a slightly used Kawasaki. With weekend liberty and his bride, Christie, on the back of the bike, Zack was loving life.

While rounding a turn on the Pacific Coast Highway, Zack lost control of the bike and crossed the centerline. Veering into the path of oncoming traffic, Zack and Christie were hit head-on. Zack died instantly but, miraculously, Christie survived.

Because of her injuries, Christie spent more than a week in the hospital and three months in a rehabilitation facility. A lot of the guys that Zack and Christie hung around with came to see her in the hospital and in rehab. Christie looked forward to their visits. They made her laugh and she felt good, at least for a few minutes.

Wade, who worked on base, came to see Christie more than the rest. He made her feel uncomfortable, although Christie couldn't put her finger on what bothered her. Whenever he was around, her female radar sent out warning signals. Wade always seemed to get too close or too personal.

One day, Wade came in smelling of alcohol, and cornered Christie as she sat in her wheelchair. Luckily, her nurse walked in at that moment. He saw what was happening, told Wade to leave her alone, and called security.

*M*ILITARY WIDOWS ARE RELUCTANT TO TALK about inappropriate advances. These advances are almost always a surprise, catch you off guard, and may make you feel guilty.

When your husband's death leaves you emotionally destroyed, it is natural to turn to others for support. You were probably comforted by a number of people, men and women who offered you a shoulder to lean on and provided some life-affirming hugs when you needed them. When confronted with death, it is natural to seek out physical touch; it provides a sense of comfort and security.

After your husband died, you probably still considered yourself to be his wife for some time. As a married woman, you likely saw your husband's male friends as "buddies," and they thought of you in the same way. Don't assume that because these guys were buddies before, however, they will remain in that big-brother role. Remember, in their eyes your identity has changed, and probably before you were ready for it. Men may now see you, a widow, as an available woman, even if you don't feel that way. Whether you like it or not, many men will view you as an attractive—and now single—woman.

WHAT ARE INAPPROPRIATE ADVANCES?

Inappropriate advances range from badly chosen comments, to a hug that lasts too long, to unwanted kissing and touching, to sexual assault or other improper behaviors. If the advance was at the low end of the scale, you may have felt embarrassed and disappointed with the friend who crossed the line. At the other end of the scale, if you were sexually assaulted, you likely felt violated and betrayed by someone you trusted when you were in need of a supportive friend.

HOW YOU ARE AT RISK

You may have thought that by being a widow, you were protected from advances. You believed that supposed friends would never take advantage of you when you were vulnerable. It is another loss when you realize the trust you placed in some of your friends was more than they deserved.

At a time when your world has already been shattered, you must keep your guard up and your female radar on. You might have a gut feeling about a person or situation, but because you are feeling so out of sorts, you find yourself disregarding these warning signals.

Sometimes your actions as a newly widowed woman are misread or misunderstood. For example, maybe one evening you want to escape from the present state of your life. You get together with friends for some laughs and a few drinks. For a few hours, it's fun to feel alive again. Maybe one of the guys, who always found you attractive, now sees you as available, and feels he needs to act before some other guy snatches you up. Fueled by alcohol, he makes some moves, with his interests—and not your feelings—foremost in his mind.

ALCOHOL IS NOT HARMLESS

You may find that having a few drinks helps you to relax. Remember, though, that too many drinks can mess with your female radar, lower your defenses, and increase your risk of becoming a victim of sexual assault. Not only is it more difficult for you to keep your wits about you, but also you are less physically able to resist someone's unwanted advances.

DATE RAPE

Sometimes a widow finds herself willingly in the arms of a man, enjoying the feeling of being with a male again. This isn't a bad thing. Perhaps all you're interested in is some physical contact, but not sex. You make this fact known to your companion, but he ignores you and presses on, becoming more aggressive and intimate. Ultimately, he forces you into a sexual act. This is rape.

If you were raped by a friend or acquaintance, you likely experienced a wide variety of feelings and reactions afterward. Because you know the assailant, you may question whether you led the guy on or gave him mixed signals. This internal questioning is normal, but keep in mind that date or acquaintance rape is still rape.

If this happened to you, you may wonder if you did all the right things to try and prevent the rape from happening. Whatever you did at that time was probably the right thing to do, because you survived the assault.

A SPECIAL CAUTION: DATE RAPE DRUGS

In recent years, date rape drugs have been increasingly used to make a woman unconscious and unable to resist unwanted advances or to accurately tell what happened the next day. Most date rape drugs are odorless and colorless. You wouldn't know that one had been slipped into your drink until it was too late. Mixed with alcohol, these drugs become highly potent weapons against you.

The following, according to a McKinley Health Center report, are the three most commonly used date rape drugs:

DRUG	STREET NAMES
Rohypnol	Roofies, Rope, Ruffies, R2, Ruffles, Roche, Forget-pill
Gamma Hydroxy Butyrate	GHB, Liquid Extacy, Liquid X, Scoop, Easy Lay
Ketamine Hcl	"K," Special "K," Ket

If you were subdued by alcohol or a date rape drug and were not aware of what was happening, you may have felt confused or uncertain about the details afterward. This is normal. Maybe you didn't initially know you were sexually assaulted but suspected that you were. You can't remember too much, or the events were blurred together. You probably felt ashamed, confused, and vulnerable. It was hard to know what to do, or perhaps you were embarrassed to tell anyone, especially because you knew the man.

A man who slips a drug into a woman's drink is a criminal. His motivation is simple: to take control and make you a victim of his advances. These men can be civilian or military and, at first, may seem respectable. This makes it easier for others to believe them later when they claim that sex was consensual. The truth is, they count on you not coming forward and pressing charges.

WHAT TO DO IF YOU ARE RAPED

Sometimes, no matter what precautions you take, you become a victim of sexual assault. This traumatic experience adds insult to injury after your husband's death. It is essential you take care of yourself, both *physically and emotionally.*

Anyone who has been sexually assaulted should be checked out medically. Call a rape crisis center immediately. You can find the phone number in the first couple of pages of your telephone book. A counselor will tell you what to do before leaving home and what to bring to the emergency room with you.

When you get to the hospital, staff members will ask whether you want to press charges. If so, medical personnel will treat you and also contact the local law-enforcement unit. The hospital staff will collect the necessary evidence. Tell them if you suspect that a date rape drug was used. The hospital will also need to check you for pregnancy and sexually transmitted diseases.

EMOTIONAL RESPONSES TO INAPPROPRIATE ADVANCES

Depending on what happened to you, you may experience a wide range of emotions. Your emotional state has already been bombarded by your husband's death, and you may find that your responses to inappropriate comments, gestures, and actions can be quite powerful or extreme.

In the case of verbal advances, you may have felt embarrassed, uncomfortable, or disappointed in the person making these comments. If you were held, kissed, or touched in ways that were undesirable or improper, you likely felt helpless, angry, or appalled that a friend would make moves on you. Sexual assault can ignite some extreme feelings of shame, fear, vulnerability, betrayal, abandonment, or wanting to die.

If you have experienced any of these feelings as a result of inappropriate advances, please get counseling. You already have enough issues to deal with, and your emotional health is too important.

Report it immediately if inappropriate advances are made by someone acting in an official military capacity. If you cannot talk with your casualty officer about the incident, contact your command chaplain, or use the chain of command. Talk to the unit commander, the commanding officer of the base or post, the regional casualty office, or the casualty director of your husband's service branch.

HOW TO PROTECT YOURSELF

Your first defense is knowing and accepting that inappropriate advances can and do happen to widows. It is an adjustment to be single again; it may have been years since you were last in this position.

Knowledge is power, and the more you know, the better protected you will be. For more information on date rape drugs and how to reduce your risk of becoming a victim of rape, check the Web sites located in appendix B at the end of this book.

★ ★ ★

Lesson Learned

Ready or not, you need to be aware of inappropriate advances and keep your guard up.

PUTTING IT ALL TOGETHER

It is important to realize that inappropriate advances occur to widows, both military and civilian. It happens more often than you imagine. Remember, men view you differently now. The more savvy you become about unwanted advances, the more you can reduce your risk of becoming a victim.

CHAPTER 19

★ ★ ★

IDENTITY THEFT

Bob and Mia

Midway through the deployment, Bob's submarine pulled into Hong Kong for a port visit. Bob was glad to get off the boat and back on terra firma for a while. He joined two of his shipmates who were going shopping for their wives. When his buddies decided to return to the boat, Bob took the Star Ferry over to the Kowloon side because he wanted to go through the night market. Needing some local currency, he stopped at a major hotel to find an ATM.

Bob was never seen alive after he left the hotel. His body was found in an alley two blocks away. Bob had apparently been mugged: he had received multiple stab wounds, and his wallet—with his military ID and credit card—was missing. With no eye-witnesses, this crime remains unsolved.

Nine months after Bob was murdered, his wife, Mia, started seeing unfamiliar charges on her credit-card statement. She called the credit-card company and discovered these charges were made overseas and also in the United States. To make matters worse, Mia discovered that new credit cards were opened in Bob's name after he died. These cards had thousands of dollars charged to them. Someone had stolen Bob's identity.

The credit-card company referred Mia to the FTC's (Federal Trade Commission's) Web site on dealing with identity theft. Following the advice on this Web site, Mia contacted one of the major credit bureaus and had a fraud alert placed on her account. She then closed the accounts that were used illegally. Mia reported this crime to her local police and filed a complaint with the FTC.

*t*HERE IS NO QUESTION ABOUT IT: when your husband dies, one of the last things you need is to become a victim of identity theft. This is something you read about regularly in the newspapers; according to the FTC, approximately 5 percent of all Americans have become victims of identity theft. But a military widow may be at special risk. If the media covered your husband's death, both your names may have been in the news, making you a perfect target for dishonest people.

The FTC Web site states that identity theft occurs when someone "uses your personal information such as your name, Social Security number, credit-card number, or other identifying information, without your permission, to commit fraud or other crimes." A person might access your existing accounts, open new charge accounts, or apply for loans in either your or your husband's name. To make matters worse, the person who commits the crime is often known to you. Individuals may steal others' identities for several reasons.

First, they cannot get credit in their own name because their own credit may have been ruined. In order to get credit, they take on another person's identity, possibly yours. In this situation, they may pay the bills on these fraudulent accounts in your name for some time. However, your credit can be tarnished if these thieves default on payments.

Second, identity thieves may assume your identity to get merchandise or services, with the intention that you, the unsuspecting victim, will bear the costs. If you don't check your monthly statements carefully, you may not be aware you are a victim until the day your credit cards reach their limit, and you learn that someone else has been using your credit-card number. Identity thieves may also open new charge accounts in your name that you are not aware of. Then, out of the blue, you may receive a collections letter demanding payment on an account you know nothing about.

TAKE STEPS TO PROTECT YOUR IDENTITY

At a time when you are already feeling vulnerable, having your identity

—or your husband's—stolen only adds insult to injury. This is a time when you need to be especially cautious about whom you trust to help you take care of your personal and financial affairs. The FTC Web site included in appendix B offers these quick tips to reduce your risk of identity theft:

- Treat your credit cards and checks like cash. Don't put them anywhere you wouldn't leave money.
- When you order new checks, have them delivered to your bank or a post office box. They are very marketable to thieves and can easily be stolen from your mailbox.
- Don't imprint your SSN on checks (military personnel sometimes do this to save time).
- Shred all credit-card information, bank statements, and utility bills, as well as all those credit-card offers you get in the mail. Incredible as it may seem, identity thieves go through garbage cans to get personal information.
- Don't respond to special offers over the phone or by e-mail. Don't give anyone personal information, such as your SSN or date of birth, unless you know the business is reliable and has a valid reason for needing it.
- Don't mail bills from your home mailbox. Deposit them in a locked mailbox or at the post office. Also, take the delivered mail out of your mailbox every day. If you're going to be away from home for several days, have a trusted neighbor pick up your mail, or have the post office hold it until you return.
- Under the Fair Credit Reporting Act, you are entitled to a free copy of your credit report. Get a copy to review your credit record and determine if there has been any questionable activity on it.
- Check your husband's credit report a few months after his death to ensure no one is using his name or credit.

IF YOU DO BECOME A VICTIM OF IDENTITY THEFT

The FTC Web site (appendix B) provides detailed information on the steps to take if you should become a victim of identity theft. They recommend the following be done immediately:

- Get in touch with the fraud department of one of the major credit bureaus and have them place a fraud alert on your account.

- Close the accounts that were used illegally.
- Report the crime to your local police.
- File a complaint with the FTC.

The sooner you learn that someone is using your identity fraudulently, the faster you can take corrective action. When you act quickly, it is easier for law enforcement to follow the paper trail, stop the process, and catch the thieves.

★ ★ ★

Lesson Learned
Neither your late husband,
nor the thief who stole his identity,
should be using your credit cards.

PUTTING IT ALL TOGETHER

If you suspect you have been a victim of identity theft, enlist someone you trust to help you get to the bottom of the problem. Don't wait. Bad news doesn't get better with age. It will not resolve itself, and it will only cause you bigger headaches down the road. Web sites that provide additional information about identity theft, ways to protect yourself and your family, and corrective actions you can take, are listed in appendix B. Remember, knowledge is power.

PART FIVE

Difficult Decisions

CHAPTER 20

★ ★ ★

WHAT NOT TO DO WITH THE SGLI

Derek and Lisa

When they first got orders to Hawaii, Derek and Lisa were thrilled. This was a once-in-a-lifetime tour, and they were going to enjoy living in paradise. The couple was living a dream, but every dream has a price. Between their student loans, the state's high cost of living, and their lifestyle, Derek and Lisa were soon heavily in debt.

Derek was an ensign in the Navy, assigned as the E-Division (Electrical) Officer on a guided missile destroyer that was in the Pearl Harbor Naval Shipyard for repair. One perfect Hawaiian morning, he was supervising the removal of an assumed dead-ended cable. The senior electrician's mate had failed to verify that no current was flowing through the cable, and it was still "live." When Derek made contact with the cable, he received an electrical shock that sent him into cardiac arrest. A shipyard corpsman initiated CPR but couldn't revive him.

Undecided about where to live after Derek's burial, Lisa stayed in Hawaii, where she had a job as an assistant buyer at the Ala Moana Shopping Center. With her income and the death benefits from the government, Lisa shouldn't have had to worry about finances. But with her "I don't care—life is short" attitude, Lisa spent quite a bit of money. Her shopping sprees didn't make her feel better. In fact, she often felt worse, because she brought her shopping bags home to an empty condo.

Lisa didn't realize how much money she was spending until the day she learned she had maxed out one of her credit cards. Thinking there was a mistake, she checked the statements for the past few months. The balance had steadily gone up and she'd been oblivious to it. Lisa wasn't sure how she'd spent so much money, but she did.

Feeling like a failure, Lisa went to her credit union, which referred her to a financial planner. The financial planner helped Lisa make a budget she could live with, a plan for paying off her debt, and a strategy for investing some of the death benefits for her future.

*W*HEN YOUR HUSBAND DIED, you received a lot of money from life insurance, the death gratuity, and possibly other federal, state, or private entitlements. In all likelihood, this totaled hundreds of thousands of dollars, probably more money than you ever imagined you would have in your lifetime. Realizing how much money you were given can be sobering. For a fleeting moment, you may have felt rich, only to have this thought replaced by guilt when you remembered why you received so much money. For many military widows, the death benefits come with strong emotional strings attached.

People sometimes do some pretty strange things when they receive large sums of money. Military widows are no exception. Because money is such a personal subject, few widows like to talk about it, especially if they are embarrassed that their death benefits have dwindled down to a few dollars. Not every military widow mismanages her finances, but when it does happen, we have to wonder, "What was she thinking?"

COMMON REACTIONS TO THE DEATH BENEFITS

Here are some of the reactions military widows wrestle with concerning the death benefits they received.

IT WAS BLOOD MONEY

Many widows are troubled, knowing they received this money because their husbands died. Some feel like they were paid off for their husband's life, as if a human life could have a price tag on it. The mere thought of the money leaves them feeling unnerved, unsettled, or offended. Many widows have said they would give back every dollar if they could just have their husbands back home again.

It takes time to sort out how you feel about receiving your husband's death benefits. If you felt the money was a form of blood money, you may find yourself reacting to it in strange ways. A few widows will ignore the money for some time, refusing to deal with it. Maybe, like other widows, you feel the need to get rid of this money, so you spend it. You may end up making some unwise, and even foolish, financial decisions.

★   ★   ★
Echo
"I knew it wasn't true,
but I felt like Judas with his thirty pieces of silver."

LIFE IS SHORT
Like many other widows, you may have been caught up in thinking that if your husband could die suddenly, so could you. In this frame of mind, you may have spent money like it was going out of style. After all, tomorrow no longer brings any guarantees. With an "I don't care" attitude, a lot of cash, and no one to answer to, you may have gone overboard and bought anything and everything, without even looking at a price tag.

More than a few widows engage in what is sometimes called "retail therapy." They go on buying sprees, hoping it will make them feel better. They invariably find the shopping spree has made them feel worse, and they end up with a lot of stuff they don't want or need.

★   ★   ★
Lesson Learned
Money can't buy happiness.

IT WILL LAST FOREVER
Maybe you were accustomed to living payday to payday, and at the end of the month, you were out of money but still had unpaid bills. Now you have more money than you ever dreamed possible. You buy something you have always wanted, perhaps a new car or truck, and realize there is still plenty of money left.

It is pretty easy to keep buying all the things you have ever wanted but could never afford. The fact of the matter, however, is that the death benefits will not last forever. If you spend money beyond your means, it will disappear much sooner than you realize. This is not an uncommon problem; some lottery winners end up heavily in debt or bankrupt after a few years.

PEOPLE COME KNOCKING

Another issue widows face and are often reluctant to talk about is the number of relatives and friends who want to borrow money from you. It is amazing how many people play on your vulnerability and seek your sympathy—and financial assistance. Banks and credit unions are in the business of loaning money; widows should not be, especially with their personal assets.

WHAT YOU SHOULD DO

Receiving a large sum of money is a lot like having extra closet space. Little by little you fill up the closet until, one day, you walk into it and realize there is no room left. The same thing can happen with your money. You can spend it in dribs and drabs, and before you know it, it's all gone. You do not want to end up in this position.

Regardless of who managed the money when your husband was alive, it is your job now. If you weren't good at managing money before you received your husband's death benefits, you will not miraculously get better on your own. But managing money is a skill that can easily be learned, and now is your time to learn it.

You are dealing with many things since your husband died, but your financial security cannot be overlooked or put off until you feel better. It is essential to make sure you identify and plan for all your short- and long-term financial needs.

Your financial status has changed significantly since your husband died. In this time of emotional turmoil, don't overreact and make careless decisions that could have a lasting impact on your financial security. It does not matter whether you have a degree in finance or cannot balance your checkbook. We recommend you get professional financial planning advice.

★　★　★
Lesson Learned
If you spend all your money now, you can't get it back.

What Financial Planning Can Do for You

Some widows think financial planning is only for rich people. Other widows feel that financial planning is all about investing, and they do not have money to invest. In reality, there are many different types of financial planning, and one of them is right for you.

Widows of all income levels can find ways to save money in the present and, with a little help, invest that money wisely for the future. Sometimes a widow has never received financial planning advice and does not know how it can help her. Here is what financial planning can do for you.

PLAN FOR THE PRESENT

- Make sure you are receiving the proper benefits and entitlements.
- Create a monthly budget that covers your "must-pay" bills and leaves you with some extra money.
- Set up a financial plan to make you debt free.
- Learn how to manage your money better.
- Start planning for major expenses.
- Bridge your present financial plan to your future spending needs.

PLAN FOR THE FUTURE

- Help you identify and plan for major expenses, such as a new car or house, or college expenses for you or your children.
- Plan for the Social Security blackout period.
- Arrange for your financial security in retirement.
- Provide ongoing advice to avoid financial pitfalls and make your money work hard for you.

Where to Get Financial Help

Let's say you have a stabbing pain in your left leg. You wouldn't ask your brother for medical advice unless he was a doctor. Even then, he would refer you to a specialist because he would want to make sure you received the best medical care available. Just as your physical health is important, so too is your financial health. Family members may be sincere in wanting to help manage your money, but unless they are financial planners, you're better off sticking with an unbiased professional. Even if they are, it is always a good idea to get a second—or possibly a third—opinion.

The VA offers free financial counseling to all beneficiaries of the SGLI.

You should have received information about this financial counseling service as part of your benefits review. If you want to learn more about this assistance, called BFCS (Beneficiary Financial Counseling Service), go to the VA Web site listed in appendix B.

Perhaps you want to talk with a financial planner in person, instead of over the phone or via e-mail. Many companies offer financial planning; we don't want to recommend any one over another. To find a professional financial planner, ask for recommendations from family and friends. Check with your bank, credit union, or insurance company, or ask around your command or church. We do suggest, though, that you talk with more than one company. Look for a company that has a recognizable name, a solid history, and an understanding of the language and culture of the military.

WHAT TO LOOK FOR IN A FINANCIAL PLANNER

It is important to choose the right financial planner because you will form a personal relationship with this individual. You want someone who will understand your personal and financial situation and put your needs first. Do not be afraid to interview this person. Talk with several financial planners before you settle on one with whom to do business. Here are some questions to keep in mind when you meet with a prospective financial planner:

- What are the financial planner's credentials? Don't be afraid to ask.
- Is this individual knowledgeable about the benefits structure provided to military widows?
- Does he or she understand the military lifestyle and speak the language of the military?
- Are you comfortable talking with this person?
- Do you feel you can trust his or her advice?
- Do you feel pressured to go along with recommendations, or to buy specific products?
- Did the planner explain your financial picture in terms you clearly understand?

PUTTING IT ALL TOGETHER

The money you received in death benefits can go a long way toward providing for a comfortable and secure financial future for you and your children. Working with a professional financial planner and developing a short- and long-term financial plan is the smart thing to do.

CHAPTER 21

★ ★ ★

WHERE TO LIVE

Alex and Marie

Alex and his wife, Marie, were living on the economy in Kahl, Germany; Alex was stationed at Fleigerhorst Airfield in Hanau. At forty-three, he was a chief warrant officer flying the UH60 Black Hawk and loving every moment of it. After twenty-two years of marriage, Alex and Marie became empty nesters when they sent their youngest daughter Stateside to attend the University of Oregon with her older brother. Although they would never tell their children, Alex and Marie enjoyed being alone in Germany, with their children on another continent.

The day before their twenty-third wedding anniversary, Alex was forward deployed to Iraq in support of Operation Iraqi Freedom. He was scheduled for a two-aircraft, nighttime passenger haul in the vicinity of Baghdad. Approximately thirty minutes into the flight, Alex's Black Hawk was catastrophically hit by a surface-to-air missile. The Black Hawk crashed in a farmer's field, killing all on board. Only partial remains could be recovered. Additionally, Alex's dog tags were found mangled and charred in the wreckage, an indication of the severity of the crash and ensuing fire.

On a cold and bleak November morning, Alex was laid to rest in Arlington National Cemetery. Unsure now of anything in her life, Marie returned to Germany. High on her worry list was where to live. In the last twenty-two years, Marie had moved eighteen times as Alex transferred from duty station to duty station. For Marie, home was wherever Alex was stationed, and all of her married life centered around the Army.

When Marie returned to Germany, there was tension in the air. Her closest squadron friends struggled with what to say to her. This disturbed Marie because these folks were like family to her and Alex. For the first time ever, Marie felt out of place at a hail and farewell. She was reduced to tears when she overheard one of the wives saying that her presence put a damper on the function.

*U*NLIKE A CIVILIAN WIDOW, you will probably relocate after your husband's death. If you are living on base or post when your husband dies, you will have to move out of quarters within a year. In the past, you could stay in base housing only up to six months, but a new ruling on deaths that occurred after May 10, 2005, extends to one year the amount of time you can receive BAH (basic allowance for housing) or remain in government quarters rent free.

Although grief experts say you shouldn't make any major decisions for at least one year, the decision to move is one you will likely have to face sooner. Currently, your household goods will be moved to another location one time, at government expense, for up to a year after your husband's death. Exceptions can be made to this one-year requirement. Contact the nearest personal property office for assistance.

Even in good times, moving is stressful. Now, regardless of how you feel, you have to orchestrate an unplanned household move. And this time, you are the one who must decide where to live. Because you are not going to another duty station, this may be the first time in years that you are making such a decision, or the first time you are making it alone. There are many factors to consider.

Almost all the time, someone in your family will want you to move back home. The thought of being taken care of when you're faced with tragedy can be appealing to some women. They go back home to live and adjust to it quite easily. Other women have discovered that being married and living away from home has changed them, and they cannot return to their hometown without some difficulty or major adjustments.

If throughout your childhood and adult life someone else chose where you would live, you may find making this decision alone, in the midst of grief, unnerving, and often a little frightening.

What you need for yourself and your children for the next few years is stability. You want a place you can call home, even though it may not feel like home without your husband. You and your children need time to heal. You need a home where you feel comfortable, safe, and secure, and a place to start rebuilding your life without your husband and their father.

★   ★   ★

Lesson Learned
You need stability for the next few years.

IMPORTANT THINGS TO CONSIDER

Here are some questions to contemplate, and answer honestly, before you plan a move for yourself and your children.

ABOUT GOING HOME

- Do I want to go home?
- Can I move back to the town where I grew up?
- What freedoms or independence will I give up if I move back there?
- How important is it that I live close to my family?
- Will I need my family's help to raise the kids?
- Do I want to be near my husband's family?

ABOUT THE MILITARY

- Do I want to be far away from all military installations?
- Do I want to be able to use the commissary, the PX or exchange, and military medicine?
- How will I handle seeing other military men in uniform if I live near a base?

ABOUT GEOGRAPHIC LOCATION AND THE COST OF LIVING

- Do weather and climate matter to me?
- Do I want to live in the country or city?
- Is this a town where I want to raise my children?

- If my children have special needs, will those needs be met there?
- Will my children get a good education in this area?
- What is the cost of living there?
- Can I afford to buy a house if I want to?
- Will I be able to get a job there?
- If I want to go back to school, are there colleges nearby?
- Are there fun recreational options for my family?

ABOUT EMOTIONAL AND SOCIAL SUPPORT
- What kind of support will I have initially?
- What kind of support will I need on an ongoing basis?
- Do I have family or good friends in this area?

Once again, talk with someone you trust about this important decision. Avoid making an impulsive one. Keep your and your children's best interests in mind when you choose a place to live. You cannot move away from your feelings of loss and sadness. They will go with you whether you pack them or not.

★   ★   ★
Lesson Learned
Wherever you move, you'll take all your emotions with you.

PUTTING IT ALL TOGETHER

If you have the luxury of time before making a move, take advantage of it; there is a lot to consider. Give yourself a year or two to get adjusted to your new surroundings. Stability is important.

If you have given your new home your best shot and you are still not comfortable, then pack up and move. After all, you are used to moving every few years.

CHAPTER 22

★ ★ ★

WHAT TO DO WITH YOUR WEDDING BANDS

Lou and Aracelli

Originally from the Philippines, Aracelli's father spent twenty years in the Navy. He always hoped his daughter would marry a Navy man and was a little disappointed when she brought home a Marine. But Lou was good to Aracelli, and that was what mattered.

Lou was a good Marine, a member of a Force Recon Company. Recon training was demanding and, at times, a bit dangerous. In preparation for deployment, the company was engaging in a live-fire, room-clearing exercise. In the midst of this exercise, someone missed a signal, and Lou suffered a fatal gunshot wound.

When the Marine Corps notified Aracelli, she became hysterical. Her CACO helped to call her family, who were visiting relatives in the Philippines. When they heard the news about Lou, her parents took the first flight back to the States.

In the first few hours after she was notified, Aracelli repeatedly asked to see Lou. When she was told she couldn't see his body yet, Aracelli became obsessed with getting Lou's wedding band back. Her CACO explained that all of his personal possessions would be returned as soon as possible. But Aracelli was adamant. Lou never took off his ring. So, if it were given back to her, it meant he was dead.

Her CACO made it his priority to retrieve the ring. Aracelli cried when she slipped it on her finger. Her fingers were tiny and Lou's ring so large, that she needed to wrap tape around it to keep it from falling off. Aracelli closed her eyes, hoping to feel Lou's presence through his ring.

*b*EFORE WE DISCUSS THE DELICATE SUBJECT of what to do with your wedding bands, we have to talk about an even more sensitive subject: your husband's ring. Because many military deaths are accidental or combat related, there may have been trauma to your husband's body, and his clothes and jewelry may have been damaged or destroyed. There is a chance his wedding band was not found and returned to you. This can be devastating. His ring is a public and personal symbol of the bond between you. After all, you were the one who slipped it on his finger when you married.

The military is sensitive to recovering and returning wedding rings. If your husband's wedding band could have been found, it would have been, and given back to you. Knowing that doesn't make it any easier. One widow, agonizing over the loss of her husband's wedding band, finally found peace by accepting that he somehow took his ring with him and has it with him in heaven.

Taking Off Your Rings

A touchy question centers on when you should take off your engagement and wedding rings. The answer is: there's no one simple answer. It is a very difficult decision, usually made for more than one reason. Neither you nor your husband ended this marriage willingly. If you had your way, you would still be married.

You may be one of the widows who took off your wedding rings almost immediately. While this may seem unsettling to some, you may have found that wearing a wedding band is too painful, a constant reminder that your husband is dead. Most widows wear their wedding rings for some time, usually months or sometimes years, after their husbands die.

What often happens is you take off your wedding rings *a little at a time.* You might take off your rings in the safety of your home, for example, but put them on when you go out in public. Or you might take them off at night to sleep, when you don't have to look at the naked ring finger on your left hand. Alternatively, you might transfer your wedding rings to your right hand, or wear either your engagement ring or wedding band by itself. You may also experiment with wearing your wedding rings in different ways on different fingers. None of them will feel especially comfortable, though.

★ ★ ★
Echo
"Everyone told me I should take off my wedding rings,
but when I did, I felt like I was betraying my husband."

Back in the old days, widows would wear their engagement and wedding rings on their right hand, signifying that they were widowed. Few people know of this practice today. It is also the custom in some European countries to wear wedding rings on the right hand. If you choose to do this, some people will think you are either European or don't know your right hand from your left. But invariably, they will think you are married.

Rest assured, it will not be a pleasant experience the first time you take off your wedding rings. It's more than not wearing a wedding ring: when you even *think* about going out in public without your wedding rings, you are admitting to yourself that your husband is dead. You are ready to take the risk and venture out as a widow. This is a part of grief work.

You may find that you will go back to wearing your wedding rings on your left hand at certain times of the year, such as around the date of your husband's death, or on your wedding anniversary. This is normal. You may need a touchstone to a shared love on these difficult dates.

★ ★ ★
Lesson Learned
You will take off your wedding rings and
put them back on many times.

WHAT TO DO WITH THE RINGS
What you do with both wedding rings, once you've taken yours off, is a personal decision. Don't rush into this decision lightly or impulsively. Mull over these ideas from other widows:

- Save the rings for your children.
- Wear your wedding band—and your husband's, if you're lucky enough to have it—on a chain.
- Resize the rings to fit on your middle finger instead of your ring finger.
- Have the stones and precious metals made into another piece of jewelry. Give yourself plenty of time before you make this decision. Once you melt down a ring, it is forever.

PUTTING IT ALL TOGETHER

Do what feels right for you. After you make a decision about your rings, do nothing for a few months. Try not to think about it. Then revisit your decision and see if it still seems like the right thing to do.

CHAPTER 23

★ ★ ★

WHAT TO DO WITH THE "I LOVE ME" WALL

Max and Kelly

It wasn't one of the better nights in their marriage, but it was one that would haunt Kelly for a very long time. An innocent discussion about starting a family turned into a heated argument. At thirty, Kelly realized her biological clock was ticking. Max, who was two years younger, wasn't ready for the responsibilities of fatherhood. Neither of them got much sleep that night. They weren't in a good mood the next morning, and they ate breakfast in stony silence. Kelly was relieved when Max finally left for the squadron.

Max was an Air Force Academy graduate. A captain, he was assigned as an instructor pilot at Laughlin AFB in Del Rio, Texas. While flying in a T-38 Talon with a student on a simulated single-engine approach, the aircraft crashed on final. The accident investigation board ruled out a likely mechanical cause and determined the accident was due to an unrecoverable student-pilot error. Unofficially, the squadron wondered why Max, a seasoned instructor pilot, was not able to recover the aircraft.

Wanting to get away from the T-38s flying around Laughlin, Kelly moved back to her hometown of Colorado Springs. Her former employer gave Kelly her old job back. She temporarily moved in with her parents.

Kelly wasn't able to leave her broken heart in Texas. Too many evenings she turned to alcohol to ease her pain. Some nights Kelly wondered if her marriage to Max even happened; she was back in her old life without a husband or a baby. On one such night, Kelly opened the box of Max's Air Force plaques and pictures. In a spark of anger, she wanted to break every picture of Max in uniform. Instead, Kelly had another drink and cried herself to sleep. She realized she couldn't deal with the box—or the memories—just yet.

*a*S YOUR HUSBAND PROGRESSED THROUGH his military career and transferred from command to command, he received a variety of awards, medals, plaques, pictures, and mementos. These highlighted his accomplishments and represented his contributions to his command, his service branch, and his country.

These commendations are usually displayed somewhere in your home and are affectionately known as the "I love me" wall. Every military home has one. Whether it's in the living room, family room, office, or stairway, there is an arrangement of plaques, letters of commendation, group shots of Soldiers or shipmates, and a variety of pictures of his Bradley, his ship, his F-16, his Black Hawk, or his office in Sasebo, Japan.

Amazingly, "I love me" wall mementos are never lost or damaged in PCS moves. They are usually put up before all the household goods are unpacked. We think there is some obscure regulation that governs the protection and immediate display of the "I love me" wall.

When your husband dies, the "I love me" wall takes on a new significance. You probably see all of his military memorabilia in a different way. Widows have quite a range of reactions to an "I love me" wall. Any or all of them are appropriate, as long as you don't start throwing plaques at the fireplace or destroying awards in a moment of anger. What to do with the "I love me" wall can be a problem. We have one rock-solid piece of advice: *Don't throw anything out!*

For some widows, throwing out or even rearranging an "I love me" wall is unthinkable. They may even add their husband's shadow box and posthumous awards to the display, creating a tribute to his life. If you have done this and find comfort in it, then it's the right thing for you.

There will come a time when you will rearrange or take down your husband's "I love me" wall, but we can't say when that will happen. You will know when it's time, though. It may come with the need to move, or the desire to redecorate. Or you may walk into the room one day, look at the wall, and simply decide: it's time. You *will* know.

★   ★   ★

Lesson Learned

Your feelings about the "I love me" wall will change over time.

When you decide to take down the "I love me" wall—whether it's three months or three years after your husband's death—the question remains of what to do with all the military mementos. Once again, we are steadfast in our advice: Don't throw anything out.

Why are we so adamant? Because the "I love me" wall represents some important aspects of your husband's life, which helped to define who he was, what he valued, and perhaps why he was willing to risk his life. The recognition was important to your husband when he was alive, so decide carefully what to do with it now that he is dead.

Here are some suggestions about how to handle the "I love me" wall when you are ready to make a change.

- Pack it up carefully and put it in the attic or basement. Use this project as part of your grief work. Clean each piece of the "I love me" wall, wrap it carefully in the paper left over from your last move, label each item, and say your good-byes as you pack it into a box.
- Save it for your kids. Your children can never get enough pieces of their dad's life. As they grow into adulthood, these mementos of their father will take on a new and deeper meaning. The wall is proof that their mythical father was a real person, and that those with whom he served liked and respected him.
- Share some of the wall with his parents, brothers and sisters, or other relatives. Your husband's parents lost a son. They were proud of him and the man he became. They will treasure all reminders of his life, including these awards and commendations.
- Display those items that remind you of good times in your life. The military was a part of your life, too. Remember the times that were special for you and your husband. These times were important back then, and they are important now. While these reminders cause

heartache now, there is a good chance they will mellow into good memories.

- Ask the guys in his command if there is something special they want. Men deal with grief differently than women do. They do feel the pain of your husband's death quite deeply, but they show it in different ways. These guys may want some of the group pictures with your husband, especially reminders of past good times.
- Donate some items to his hometown elementary or high school. Schools often have displays that honor their alumni and provide valuable lessons for the school's current students. Check with your husband's schools. They may jump at the chance to honor his memory and teach their students about duty, honor, and service to country.
- Donate it to a local military museum. Every military town has at least one military museum nearby, and they are always interested in obtaining artifacts and mementos. If they can't use your husband's mementos, they might be able to suggest other organizations or retired military associations who can.

PUTTING IT ALL TOGETHER

Whatever you decide to do with the "I love me" wall, don't act in haste or in anger. Your feelings will change, and you may regret giving away your husband's awards. You may not be able to get them back if you change your mind.

PART SIX

Everyday Coping

CHAPTER 24

★ ★ ★

COPING WITH SIGNIFICANT DATES

Don and Colleen

Don was a career Soldier who saw combat in Kuwait during the First Gulf War. When he got back to the States in 1991, Don married his longtime girlfriend, Colleen, in an elaborate wedding in Knoxville, Tennessee. They had two children, Kate and Bill. Don had a break in service from 1994 to 1998. During this time, he realized that he was a Soldier at heart and reenlisted in the Army.

Don, a staff sergeant, was on a three-year recruiting assignment in Salinas, California. Recruiting duty is extremely stressful and proves difficult for many Soldiers. But Don was successful for his first two years, achieving every monthly recruiting goal. In his last year, however, the command climate changed significantly with the arrival of a new battalion commander and the difficulty all recruiters faced nationwide because of the war in Iraq.

When Don didn't make his recruiting goals in four successive months, he was counseled that his diminished performance could harm his chances for promotion. This would kill his career and his dream of becoming a command sergeant major.

With this increased stress, Don and Colleen began to have domestic problems. He came home late a few nights each week, and Colleen became suspicious, thinking he was having an affair. In reality, Don was beating the bushes, trying to attain his monthly goal.

To make matters worse, Don began to drink. Because of his drinking, he missed some recruiting appointments, which put him further behind. For the first time in his life, Don felt like a failure and couldn't see a way out of his predicament.

One Tuesday afternoon, when Colleen returned home from her job at her children's school, she found Don in the garage, dead from a self-inflicted gunshot wound. To Colleen, Don had seemed more stressed than depressed and gave no obvious signs that he was contemplating suicide. He left Colleen a brief note that simply said, "I'm sorry, but you'll be better off without me."

Don's death occurred just two days before Thanksgiving. Through the blur of the funeral, Thanksgiving came and went unobserved; Colleen and her children had little to be thankful for. The Christmas holidays, usually a season of great fun for the family, were ignored.

In many ways, the second Thanksgiving and Christmas after Don's suicide were even harder on Colleen and the kids. Wanting to run away, they rented a cabin in Vermont for Christmas week and spent the entire time skiing. By the end of each day, they were too tired to think about anything but food and a comfortable bed.

*t*HE LIST OF SIGNIFICANT DATES is long and painful. There are the old standards of Thanksgiving, Christmas, Hanukkah, and Valentine's Day, but, since you were widowed, your birthday, your husband's birthday, your wedding anniversary, and the date your husband died have all taken on a new and heartbreaking significance. They have become reminders that he is no longer around.

HANDLING SIGNIFICANT DATES

The first year after your husband dies is filled with many dreaded firsts. Weeks beforehand, you start thinking about the approaching day and obsess over all sorts of things related to it. You think back to last year, when he was alive, remembering what you said and did together. You recall that he promised he would make up for the holidays he missed while he was deployed or TDY (temporary duty). Many nights, you're awake at three in the morning, wondering how you're going to survive the significant date that is fast approaching.

★ ★ ★
Echo
"Our wedding anniversary had been a happy occasion.
Now, it measures our years of separation."

It is the little things that are personally and privately painful. You may get a dozen cards on your birthday, but you won't get the one that starts out, "To My Wife. . . ." As for his birthday, forget it. Maybe his mother will mention the date, but it will be an awkward moment. Your wedding anniversary is even worse. It will probably be ignored. No one is going to remind you that it's your anniversary—as if you could forget it.

We have two simple pieces of advice for surviving these significant dates: Do something nice for yourself and have a plan for the day.

On the days that are hard for you, make an effort to do something nice for yourself. Make an appointment for a manicure and splurge for a pedicure. Treat yourself to an extra-long massage. Go out to your favorite restaurant with friends. Order your favorite comfort food and have dessert. You deserve to be spoiled on these tough days.

If you have a plan for the day, you know what to expect—more or less. You are less likely to be caught off guard. Once this significant day is over, you will realize that you survived it, and it wasn't as bad as you thought it would be.

★ ★ ★
Lesson Learned
The days leading up to a significant date
are worse than the day itself.

SURVIVING THE HOLIDAYS

Let's be honest: the holidays were stressful even back in your old life. Widowhood adds a dimension of distress, however, that can make these occasions downright unbearable. Remember that your emotions may be pretty raw now. Whatever progress you have made toward feeling better may disappear with the approach of the holidays. This is normal. However, it may surprise you to learn that, after the holidays, you will probably bounce back, and you may even gain some ground on feeling better.

A lot about the holidays can make a widow want to scream. Some stores start putting up their Christmas decorations in August, subjecting you to four months of reminders that your husband won't "be home for Christmas." Every decorated house, Christmas tree, television commercial, and newspaper ad stabs you through the heart. If you are widowed with children, you will see happy families everywhere. If you are widowed without children, you will feel the world is populated with couples while you are conspicuously alone.

★ ★ ★

Echo
"I just barely made it through Thanksgiving. Maybe I can sleep until Christmas is over and wake up in January."

TIPS FOR HOLIDAY SURVIVAL

You can run from the holidays, but you can't hide from your emotions. Holidays were meant to be shared, so the trick is to figure out ways to survive them.

GRIEF ZAPS YOUR ENERGY, SO BE GOOD TO YOURSELF

- Eat properly.
- Do what it takes to relax—listen to music, exercise, soak in the tub.
- Get plenty of rest.
- Shop by mail or online. If you must go to the mall, shop at off-peak hours when there is less of a crowd. Give gift certificates—you won't have to wrap them.
- Keep a journal of your thoughts and feelings. If you don't like to write, buy a cheap tape recorder and a few tapes. Keep them in the car or by your bed.
- Give yourself permission to be nice to yourself.
- Attend a support group. You are not alone in dreading the holidays.
- Minimize the use of alcohol; it's a depressant.

CHOOSE TO DECORATE LESS

- If you have kids, decorating is a must, but don't tire yourself out.
- Put up only those decorations you can tolerate for a few weeks.
- Decorate wisely, remembering it also takes energy to undecorate.

CHRISTMAS CARDS

- Skip them if it's too painful.
- It you want to stay in touch with friends, write later in the year.

SOCIAL EVENTS

- Know your limits. It's okay to say, "Not this year."
- Surround yourself with sensitive and supportive people.
- Minimize contact with negative people, even if they are family members.
- Tell your hostess you may cancel at the last minute if you don't feel up to going out. Widows have a right to be unpredictable.
- Make an appearance; then decide if you want to stay longer.

HOLIDAY MEALS

- Change the usual time and menu for dinner.
- Avoid an empty seat by rearranging places at the table.
- Try a potluck dinner to avoid having to cook.
- Order take-out.
- Buy paper plates to minimize the cleanup.
- Be a guest, not a hostess.
- Eat out.

REMEMBER YOUR LOVED ONE

- It's okay to put up his Christmas stocking.
- Share good memories of your husband with your kids.
- Do something special for you and your family in his memory.
- Start a new tradition.

HELP OTHERS IN NEED

- Help out at a soup kitchen or food bank.
- Visit a nursing home.
- Volunteer at an SPCA shelter.

★ ★ ★
Lesson Learned
*What you do to survive the first set of holidays
is probably not what you'll do next year.*

PUTTING IT ALL TOGETHER

Surviving your first set of holidays and significant dates is tough. The good news is they get easier, once you know what to expect. Having lived through them once, you can do it again. How you deal with significant dates will change in the future as you adjust to life without your husband.

CHAPTER 25

★　★　★

WIDOW HUMOR

Bret and Stephanie

Bret and Stephanie were an easy-going, fun-loving, and sociable couple. With a sparkle in his eyes and his mustached grin, Bret always had a joke to tell. Stephanie's humor was drier than her husband's, but both could easily make others laugh and were fun to have around.

Stationed in Italy, Bret flew helicopters in the Navy, while Stephanie worked for the Department of Defense on base. After this tour, they hoped to return Stateside and start a family. But right now, Bret and Stephanie's life was carefree and fun.

In mid-February, Bret and another pilot were tasked to ferry replacement parts and two aviation mechanics to a downed squadron helicopter. While flying VFR (visual flight rules), Bret and his copilot encountered some unpredicted weather. Wanting to complete the mission, the pilots decided to press on. The weather conditions deteriorated rapidly, and in worsening visibility, the helicopter flew into an unlit communications tower. All six souls on board were lost.

After the crash, Stephanie relocated to northern Virginia. She knew she wasn't herself when she didn't complain about the daily commute into the Pentagon.

Stephanie thought her sense of humor died with Bret. She no longer read the comics in the newspaper or watched the comedy shows she used to enjoy with him. As the months slipped by,

Stephanie became tired of feeling bad. She started to find humor in her life again, but not like before. Now she was making fun of life, death, and widowhood. Stephanie found a small sense of control in her dark humor, and she liked that feeling.

Stephanie quickly learned, however, that most people don't understand or appreciate widow humor. They expected reverence and respect from her, not jokes about dead husbands.

*Y*OU WON'T FIND A SELECTION OF humorous sympathy cards in your local card shop. There is no book called *101 Funny Things to Say at a Funeral* in any library. You don't hear the late-night talk show hosts make jokes about death and grief. Yet, put a few military widows together, and without even trying, some pretty irreverent humor comes out.

Widows have a tendency to make jokes about subjects that the average person only speaks about in hushed and reverent tones. To the non-widowed, death is serious stuff, and there is not too much to laugh at, unless, of course, you have lived through it—if you'll pardon the pun.

WIDOW HUMOR?

As every widow knows, you reach a point where you can't stand the dreariness of grief any longer, and you start to make fun of your current life—death and all. In some ways, making fun of death and widowhood is liberating. It gives you a breather from the weight that widowhood places on your shoulders. Humor allows you to escape from grief and feel good. It connects you with life again.

Humor can also give you a certain sense of control at a time when you have little control in your life. It is a sign that you are taking action to make your life a little more tolerable. Humor is a sign of hope.

★   ★   ★

Lesson Learned
Humor helps you cope with the insanity of widowhood.

Widow humor has a dark side. It can be caustic, flippant, morbid, mocking, sacrilegious, and at times profane. There aren't too many people who appreciate widow humor. In fact, it is only marginally tolerated by most people.

In reality, widow humor is not all that unusual. It's similar to the gallows humor people use when they work in high-risk occupations or deal with traumatic or extreme life-threatening situations on a regular basis. There is something about working with death that makes you want to poke fun at it. It's the same with widowhood.

RULES FOR USE OF WIDOW HUMOR

Widow humor should not be used outside of the surroundings where it is understood and accepted. To make sure you aren't labeled as unfeeling or irreverent, we have put together some rules for using widow humor:
- Only *you* can make fun of certain subjects, like dead husbands.
- You won't like it if a non-widow uses widow humor.
- Not every widow will appreciate your humor.
- Some of your humor may be taken as morbid, disrespectful, or insensitive, even by other widows.
- Widow humor is incredibly personal.
- Non-widowed people won't get it.

Only a seemingly disturbed individual would deliberately poke fun at death, grief, and widowhood. Unless, of course, you've been there, done that, and understand it as only a miltary widow can!

We have opted not to include examples of widow humor, not because we don't have some real gems, but simply because what we find funny may not be amusing to you. So we will keep them to ourselves, smile, and laugh at some odd and maybe even inappropriate times. You know what we mean.

THE POSITIVE BENEFITS OF HUMOR

A popular school of thought says that humor has many benefits. Many years ago, Norman Cousins, the former editor of the *Saturday Review of Literature*, wrote *Anatomy of an Illness as Perceived by the Patient* (1979). In it, he described how he survived a condition called ankylosing spondylitis, a rare connective tissue disease. His odds of recovery were five hundred to one. When the doctors could offer little relief from his pain with conventional treatment, Cousins decided to pursue a very unorthodox remedy. He took high doses of vitamin C and checked into a hotel room, where he watched Marx brothers movies over and over again (Read-Brown).

Cousins found that, after hours of laughing, not only did he sleep better, but he also needed less pain medication. He attributed his recovery to the positive effects of laughter, a good attitude, and his dietary regimen. While the verdict is still out on what helped him get better, there has since been a great deal of research on humor and its positive effects on our minds and spirits.

We know from experience that laughter, like tears, is great for releasing the tensions that build up inside us. Sometimes we don't know whether to laugh or cry. For example, we have all experienced a good laughing jag after hearing a joke that wasn't really funny, yet, we couldn't stop laughing. It made us feel good, both while we were laughing and afterward.

Here are some other good things that humor and solid laughter can do for you, adapted from *How Stuff Works* (McGhee, 1998). Humor can:

- reduce the production of stress hormones in your body;
- have cardiovascular benefits (science has shown that one hundred good laughs provide the same benefit as fifteen minutes on a rowing machine. Some refer to this benefit as "internal jogging" —who knew?);
- help relieve pain;
- improve your resistance to illness;
- help cleanse your lungs of old air and move fresher air in;
- promote relaxation by helping to circulate your blood and improve your muscle tone; and
- result in a sense of well-being by counteracting other emotions, such as anxiety or fear.

We have talked about the positive benefits of humor. Are there any negative effects? None that we know of—except people may think you're nuts for making jokes about life, death, and widowhood.

PUTTING IT ALL TOGETHER

Laughter is a great way to release tensions and the buildup of emotions that accompany any stressful situation. Some people may not appreciate widow humor, but don't let that stop you from using it.

CHAPTER 26

★ ★ ★

STAYING HEALTHY WHILE GRIEVING

Gary and Erin

Gary was a communications systems sergeant stationed at Fort Huachuca in Arizona. He and Erin had been married four years. They had an eighteen-month-old son and a daughter on the way, due to make her arrival in about three months.

Gary was supposed to pick up diapers at the commissary before he left post, but he forgot and arrived home without them. Right after dinner, while Erin was giving their son a bath, Gary dashed up to the local convenience store for the diapers. Little did he know he was walking into danger—an armed robbery was in progress.

The sound of the opening door startled the robber, who swung around and shot Gary point-blank. He then stepped over Gary's body and made his escape. The entire episode was captured on the store's surveillance tape. The suspect was caught a few hours later and charged with murder, armed robbery, and illegal drug possession.

Before Gary's murder, Erin had been in excellent heath and had had an uneventful pregnancy. The news of Gary's death put her into an emotional and physical tailspin. Erin was relieved when her mother, Carol, offered to come and take care of her. In fact, as soon as she got the call about her son-in-law's death, she started packing. A nurse, Carol immediately took charge of her daughter, her grandson, and the household.

Carol made sure Erin saw her obstetrician immediately. The doctor decided to monitor Erin's blood pressure frequently and advised her to stay off her feet. Erin was terrified that she would lose this little girl, the last child she and Gary would have together. Determined to carry her baby to term, Erin followed the doctor's instructions to the letter. She got out of bed only to attend Gary's funeral and memorial service.

Erin found that even though she had no appetite she ate the healthy meals her mother made for her baby's sake. While she had no control over Gary's murder, Erin wasn't going to let there be a second fatality from this terrible crime by losing their unborn child.

*W*E EXPLAINED EARLIER IN THIS BOOK that loss and other stressors can affect your physical health. In this chapter, we will talk about several other ways that stress can affect your mind and body. We will also discuss steps you can take to maintain your physical and emotional health during this difficult time.

EFFECTS OF STRESS ON YOUR MIND AND BODY

Even if you were relatively healthy when your husband died, the effect of his death can be overwhelming to your physical and emotional well-being. Indeed, it would be strange if your body did not mirror the strong feelings of stress you are having. For example, you may have noticed changes in your skin and hair, your digestive system, or your menstrual cycle. Don't hesitate to discuss these physical changes with your doctor. Your body was designed to try and correct itself whenever one part is not working as well as it should. But in times of continual stress, it often needs medical attention.

The paragraphs that follow describe some common physical problems widows experience.

YOU HAVE PROBLEMS SLEEPING

You are probably having a great deal of trouble falling and staying asleep. This is a common problem for widows and other people who have suffered sudden and traumatic losses. You may find that your mind can't settle down enough to fall asleep. Or, you may fall asleep but wake up in the middle of the night, or too early in the morning. Your sleep may also be interrupted by bad dreams or nightmares. A good night's sleep is essential to your physical and emotional health. If you are having trouble sleeping, please talk with a doctor.

YOU HAVE NO ENERGY

Under normal circumstances, your body will store up simplified sugar from food to give you a ready source of energy when you need it. When you are coping with very stressful situations, however, your body will produce more adrenalin. Adrenalin helps you cope better with whatever is causing you stress. It does this, among other ways, by sending a signal to your liver, telling it to release its stored sugar so your body will have the energy it needs. When you are under extreme stress, your body continues to manufacture adrenalin. Your liver has no time to recover and store more energy. When this happens, you will constantly feel tired—like you are having your own internal "energy crisis."

YOU HAVE NO RESISTANCE TO ILLNESS

Along with feeling continually tired, you may find you are more susceptible to colds, flu, and other illnesses that your body might ordinarily ward off. This is because continuous and overwhelming stress lowers your resistance to illness. Your body finds it difficult to keep up a battle on two fronts—the one you are fighting to hold your emotions and spirit together, and the one against potential illnesses. When your resistance goes down during stressful times, it is much easier to get sick.

WHAT YOU CAN DO TO HELP YOURSELF

The bottom line is this: your body demands more attention to keep going and stay well. If your body is run down and you have no energy, your brain, likewise, will not have what it needs to help you think straight. Here are some ways to help you get your strength back and feel better. These suggestions will fall into the categories of—no surprise—diet, exercise, and relaxation techniques.

DIET

We are not talking about a diet to lose weight, although many widows have described the "magical twenty pounds" they either gained or lost after their husbands' die. Rather, consider food as the fuel you need in order for you to deal with what you are going through. You may be telling yourself, "I just can't eat anything," and skip meals. Maybe you are constantly eating comfort food, or surviving on fast food, coffee, alcohol, or cigarettes. Long term, these eating habits will not keep you healthy.

Physically, you may feel you are a shadow of your former self. Eating a balanced diet will not take away your grief, but it will help you to keep your energy up and cope better with the tiredness and exhaustion.

The new food pyramid, recently published by the USDA (U.S. Department of Agriculture), promotes a balanced lifestyle that incorporates healthy eating habits and exercise. The Web site for the USDA is found in appendix B.

★　★　★

Lesson Learned
Chocolate isn't a food group.

EXERCISE

Working out can go a long way toward helping you to deal with ongoing stress. Not only will it help you sleep better, it is also a good way to work off the physical tension and emotions that seem to ebb and flow so strongly since your husband died.

Exercise can also help you to regulate your blood sugar—a problem for people under stress. Additionally, it helps you to keep your body and your spirit connected. Remember to check with your doctor before starting an exercise program.

RELAXATION TECHNIQUES

Perhaps you are already using relaxation strategies. If so, good for you. Now, think of these techniques as a way to do something nice for yourself and help you to cope with the strong emotions that are now part of your life.

One of the easiest techniques you can use to relax is breathing exercises. Regulating your breathing can help to calm your body. It has been found that if you calm your body, you can also calm your mind. Breathing exercises are especially useful when you are trying to fall asleep or when you must deal with tough emotions during the day.

A simple breathing exercise consists of sitting comfortably on a chair or couch with your feet flat on the floor. Take one hand and hold one side of your nose closed while you breathe in slowly through the other side. When you are finished breathing in, hold your breath a few seconds and, slowly, breathe out through your mouth through pursed lips (form your lips like you're blowing up a balloon). Repeat several times, alternating the side of your nose. You should feel calmer.

Hot baths are a great way to decompress: they can help to relax your muscles and get rid of the tension that builds up in them. They are especially helpful after a long day or near bedtime.

Think about treating yourself to a massage. If you have ever had one, you know the benefits. If you haven't, this is a good time to try it.

Finally, there are lots of other ways to relax: meditation, yoga, or tai chi. Go with whatever works for you. Don't be afraid to try something new.

★   ★   ★

Echo
"Sometimes, the highlight of my day is
my fifteen-minute soak in the tub."

IF YOU WERE DIAGNOSED WITH A CHRONIC ILLNESS BEFORE YOUR HUSBAND DIED

Some illnesses are strongly affected by stress. Good examples are multiple sclerosis or manic depression. With chronic illnesses, the severity of your symptoms can escalate or change, depending upon what is going on in your life.

You may have felt your condition was under control. Then, suddenly, your husband died. Maybe you found that, quite unexpectedly, the symptoms of your illness flared up. If you are diabetic, you might have needed to check your blood sugar more frequently to keep it even.

If you had a chronic illness before your husband died, you probably need to stay in frequent contact with your doctor. Ask him to monitor you more closely until your condition has restabilized.

PUTTING IT ALL TOGETHER

The stress associated with trauma and grief often has a strong impact on your physical health. While your body tries to adapt to these stressful times, you can do a lot to help yourself. Diet, exercise, and relaxation techniques can help you to manage the impact of loss and trauma. If you had been diagnosed with a chronic illness before your husband died, it is especially important to stay in touch with your doctor and have your condition closely followed.

CHAPTER 27

★ ★ ★

IN-LAWS, EX-WIVES, AND STEPCHILDREN

Eric and Emily

Eric and Emily met one Sunday morning in sunny Southern California while they were on a local bike club's fifty-mile ride. Swerving to avoid a crazy driver, Eric lost control of his bike and ran into an old, and very large, tree. Embarrassed by his accident, Eric was mortified when he learned that the woman with whom he was flirting was the doctor who took charge of getting him to a hospital.

Eric was captivated by more than Emily's bedside manner, and a year and a half later, they were married. Eric's family adored Emily. His mother and father were absolutely delighted when the newlyweds announced they hoped to make them grandparents very soon.

Their plans to start a family were changed when Eric's Marine reserve unit was activated, and he received orders to the Middle East. An officer in the California Highway Patrol in civilian life, Eric had just pinned on the gold oak leaves of a major in the Marine Corps.

Over in Iraq, as the operations officer of his battalion, Eric's primary duties were in the relatively safe command post. But as a Marine, he had been trained to lead from the front and he occasionally accompanied patrols.

Several days before the Iraqi elections, Eric and his Marines were on patrol in the city of Fallujah when they were ambushed by insurgents looking to disrupt the elections. The ambush was initiated with an IED (improvised explosive device), followed by small-arms fire. As the gunners returned fire from the turrets of their armored Humvees, the rest of the Marines dismounted to clear the ambush.

While there were no obvious signs of rank on Eric's uniform, perhaps it was the manner in which he took charge that drew the sniper's attention to him. Eric died instantly from the shot.

Emily and Eric's parents were all deeply hurting, but each faced a different loss. Emily lost her husband, the love of her life. Eric's parents lost a child, their firstborn son.

Emily was grateful she had his family nearby. She relied on them heavily in the months after Eric's death. While his parents were devastated by the death of their son, they made a special effort to help Emily, whom they loved like a daughter.

*a*LL OF THE RELATIONSHIPS you have will be strained by the death of your husband. In this chapter, we will look at how the ways you relate to your in-laws, your husband's ex-wife, and your stepchildren will change now that you are a widow.

IN-LAWS

Some widows wonder if they are still related to their in-laws after their husband's death. We don't know the legal answer, but your in-laws are your late husband's parents, so from our perspective, they are still family. What will change is your relationship. It has to change, because one of the key players, your husband, is no longer a part of that unique foursome of son and daughter-in-law, and mother- and father-in-law.

Before your husband died, your relationship with your in-laws generally fell into one of three categories. In the first category, you had a terrific relationship with your husband's parents, and you were a welcomed and well-loved member of their family. In the second category, you and your in-laws had a civil and polite relationship, but you didn't have a genuine connection. In the last category, your relationship with your in-laws was tense and strained. Your connection was an obligatory one. In essence, you were related only because you married their son.

WORDS OF CAUTION

If you saw your in-laws just a few times a year when your husband was alive, be aware that the first few times you see them after his death may be unnerving. You may never have noticed the traits, features, mannerisms, or quirky habits that your husband had in common with his parents. These characteristics and similarities have always been there, but now they jump out at you. They can catch you off guard and make you miss your husband more—if that's possible.

You may notice that your husband got his smile and the sparkle in his eyes from his mother. Or your father-in-law sounds hauntingly like your husband when he leaves you voice mail. You might walk into a room and see him sitting in the recliner in exactly the same position your husband sat in. Perhaps you thought your husband was the only person in America who didn't put milk on his cereal, until you had breakfast with his brother. Oh, those quirky habits!

At first, it may be painful to see little bits of your husband in his parents or siblings. But, as time wears away the jagged edges of your grief, you will find these familial reminders comforting.

DIFFERENT LOSSES

It is important to remember that you and your husband's family are deeply hurting, but you are hurting in different ways. You all lost the same man, but he had different roles in your lives.

You lost a husband, someone whom you loved in the many ways in which women love the men they marry. You made a life with this man and most likely created a family with him. He represented many things to you; he was your present and future world.

Your in-laws lost a son, which is much different from losing a husband. Remember that with biological children, there was never a time in your husband's life that his parents were not a part of it. Your in-laws lost the baby they created, the little boy they raised into a man they were proud of, and the son they thought would take care of them in their later years.

PARENTAL GRIEF

Many books have been written on the subject of parental grief, and so our purpose is just to give you a basic understanding of what your in-laws are going through. The grief they feel for their lost son is acutely intense.

For a parent to outlive a child is a violation of the laws of nature. It defies every hope, dream, and expectation parents have for their children. It was your in-laws' worst nightmare to bury their son.

Parental grief is complicated. It takes a very long time for parents to work through the essential tasks of grieving a child, even an adult one. Some parents are never able to find peace after their child's death, especially if the death was sudden and the circumstances were complex, as sometimes happens in war, accidents, homicides, and suicides. It is often a lifetime struggle for parents to adapt to a world without their child.

Losing a child, even an adult one, can produce extreme but different reactions in a mother and a father. The reason is that men grieve differently than women. While your mother-in-law may be reduced to uncontrollable tears by the sight of her son's favorite coffee mug, your father-in-law may want to fix things around your house.

We know of one father who, after viewing the wreckage of his son's aircraft, spent the rest of a hot summer's day massacring bushes with hedge clippers. In his own way, he was doing grief work. He worked off his frustration physically by exercising control over the poor, unsuspecting hedges, which needed a trimming but got a "high and tight." This grieving father could not protect his son from death, but he could control the size of the bushes.

Sometimes, parental grief can be disenfranchised. As an example, if all the attention was focused on you and your children at the funeral, your in-laws may have felt they did not receive the level of sympathy and comfort they needed and deserved. They may have felt their loss was minimized and seen as secondary to yours. Just because their son was married, with a family of his own, does not mean your in-laws hurt less over his death.

Parental grief can be overlooked in our society. For example, when your husband died, you became his widow. When children lose both parents, they are called orphans. However, there is no term to describe the parent whose child has died.

A NEW RELATIONSHIP WITH YOUR IN-LAWS

No matter what your previous relationship was with your in-laws, the death of your husband changed its nature. If you had a good relationship with them, then it will probably continue to be good. If you think of your husband's family as your own, there is no reason why they cannot remain a vital part of your life.

It is possible to have a good relationship with your in-laws and still move forward with your life. We know of one military widow who asked her mother-in-law to be her matron of honor when she considered getting married again.

If your relationship with your in-laws was lukewarm, this may be the time to make some positive changes. You have both lost someone you loved very much, and you can find comfort and strength for yourself and your children in your husband's family. Your in-laws will want to continue to see their grandchildren, and rightfully so; they are the children of their son.

This may be the time to bury the hatchet and work out a relationship with your husband's family for the sake of the kids. You don't want your children to suffer another loss by denying them a relationship with their grandparents. Try looking for common ground with your in-laws. Perhaps a better relationship will grow out of your shared loss.

If your relationship with your in-laws was a rocky one, usually it will not get better. Often there are some underlying issues nagging at all of you. If so, your husband's death may only make a bad situation worse. Most likely, you and your in-laws will go your separate ways. The issues that caused conflict in your relationship will never be discussed, much less resolved.

Remember: grief does not bring out the best in anyone. We hope neither you nor your in-laws will burn any bridges. Neither of you needs any more hurt in your life. Leave the door open for a better relationship. You may feel differently about each other in a few years.

★ ★ ★
Lesson Learned
Your in-laws' greatest fear came true when their son died.

EX-WIVES

If your husband had an ex-wife, in all likelihood she will reenter the picture soon after his death. In fairness to ex-wives, not all of them are troublesome. But we have noticed that the more recent her divorce from your husband is, the less likely the emotional dust of the divorce has settled, and the more likely you'll have hard feelings toward her—and vice versa. As a result, you'd probably prefer not to have her around, especially in this emotionally volatile time.

Ex-wives have a way of showing up uninvited, and they usually bring along a good bit of baggage. They often come to the funeral and the military memorial service, sometimes acting like a bereaved family member instead of keeping a low and respectful profile. This can be upsetting and appear hypocritical, especially if she behaved badly toward your husband when he was alive.

Even if you had a tolerable relationship with your husband's ex-wife, probably you and your husband's family did not want to see her at the funeral or be forced to make small talk with her at the reception afterward. We know of one ex-wife who, immediately after the command memorial service, had the nerve to ask the widow if she would still be receiving child support.

An ex-wife often thinks she is entitled to something after your husband's death. Usually, it's money. Too many ex-wives feel that either you or the military owes them some monetary payment for their years of marriage. They overlook the "ex" in ex-wife.

★ ★ ★

Echo
"It's just like his ex to think only of herself, forgetting,
once again, that I am his wife."

For your own sake, avoiding conflicts and confrontations with your husband's ex-wife is the right thing to do. If there are issues that must be resolved between you, we suggest using an intermediary: a family member, a trusted friend, or an attorney. As we said earlier, grief doesn't bring out the best in anyone, so unless you are good friends, let someone else deal with your husband's ex-wife.

On the subject of money, there are some circumstances where your husband's ex-wife may legally be entitled to receive his Social Security benefits. If the ex-wife is unmarried and the legal guardian of his dependent children under the age of sixteen, she can receive Social Security for herself while the children are minors.

Every once in a while, an ex-wife has received a former husband's SGLI. Usually, under these circumstances, the service member had neglected to name you, his new wife, as the beneficiary on his life insurance policy. This happens more often than you would imagine.

People tend to shy away from taking care of such sobering topics as life insurance. If your husband forgot to change his SGLI beneficiary, and his ex-wife, or someone else, received the insurance money, you know what a problem it can be. Remember that the SGLI is a legal contract and not a benefit, such as Social Security or the DIC (Dependency and Indemnity Compensation) from the VA. The military must abide by the contract. If someone other than yourself was named as your husband's life insurance beneficiary, you may want to talk with a lawyer about potential legal options.

STEPCHILDREN

If you were a stepmother to your husband's children, you can count on this relationship changing, too. If the stepkids lived with you and your husband, they will probably go back to living with their biological mother. They may want to continue living with you, especially if they have lived with you and your husband for some time. They may feel comfortable in your home, have half-brothers or -sisters there, or go to a school they like.

If you did not adopt your husband's children, you have few legal rights. Our system favors the biological parent as the children's legal guardian. It is a secondary loss when the stepchildren you cared for on a daily basis are taken away from you. Another part of your old life is gone. Once again, it's out of your control.

Sometimes, a biological mother may cut off communication between you and the stepkids, deciding you don't have a place in their lives. It may surprise you how difficult this loss can be, but remember, you have lost another connection to your husband.

If you are allowed continued contact with your stepkids, keep in mind that they are also grieving. They may not know what grief is, or how to show what they are feeling. They are still kids, and they do not have the maturity or coping skills that many adults have developed.

Beginning with their parents' divorce and then the death of their father, these kids have suffered some major losses in their young lives. They may blame themselves, or possibly you, for their parents' divorce or their father's death. You can be the perfect target for their anger. In their minds, they can't be mad at their father without feeling guilty, nor can they be mad at their mother, their only remaining biological parent. The good relationship you had with them can instantly go up in smoke.

If your husband's children do not live with you, they will have their own casualty officer; dependent children are entitled to government benefits, too. Their benefits are separate and distinct from yours and in no way affect the compensation you receive from the government. Whatever provisions your husband made for his children in his will is another matter.

PUTTING IT ALL TOGETHER

Your relationships with your husband's parents, his children, and other family members will probably change in significant ways. Try not to burn any bridges right after your husband's death, although we know that relationships with in-laws, ex-wives, and stepchildren were often kept alive because of him. There will be time to sort out these relationships in the months and years ahead, when emotions have had time to settle down, and everyone is thinking a bit more clearly.

CHAPTER 28

★ ★ ★

DATING AGAIN

Sam and Aurora

Sam was a lieutenant colonel and an intelligence officer in the Air Force. For the past three years, he had been assigned as a joint service officer at Headquarters Central Command at MacDill AFB in Tampa, Florida.

Without warning, Sam began to have bad headaches and bouts of dizziness. He dismissed them as stress. Sam figured his upcoming dive trip to Belize with his wife, Aurora, was all he needed to feel better. On the day before his leave began, Sam had a seizure in his office. The paramedics took Sam to the base hospital. He was undergoing a CT scan when Aurora arrived.

The news was grim. Sam had a metastatic brain tumor. Because his condition was advanced, there was little hope of recovery. As the cancer continued to spread, Aurora had a hard time watching her athletic husband wither away to skin and bones. Less than four months after Sam's diagnosis, Aurora buried him. At thirty-eight, she became a widow with two teenagers to raise.

Aurora didn't know where the next two years went. She was now facing forty, nearing menopause, and having a midlife crisis. Although she still missed Sam, Aurora was lonely for adult male attention. Her kids had a fit when she casually mentioned that one of the men in her office invited her to lunch. They couldn't picture her with anyone except their father. And besides, they thought, she was too old to date.

Sometimes Aurora wondered if her kids were right. She hadn't dated in eighteen years, and she wasn't sure where to start. The thought of dating scared her, but the thought of living alone for the rest of her life terrified her even more. Aurora decided to accept her colleague's invitation for lunch sometime soon.

*d*ATING AFTER YOUR HUSBAND'S DEATH is different from dating when you were single or after getting divorced. If you are like most military widows, you probably dread getting back into the singles' world again. If you were married a short time, you remember the trials and tribulations of finding a good man. If you were married for a number of years, the thought of dating may fill you with terror. In either situation, dating produces lots of anxiety.

FAMILY AND FRIENDS

In all likelihood, friends or family brought up the subject of remarriage soon after your husband died, sometimes within the first few days or weeks. If this happened to you, it probably came as a shock, and perhaps you were offended. They did not mean to be offensive. They wanted to fix your grief.

Because you are a young widow, your family and friends looked upon your husband's death as especially tragic. They hate seeing you alone and watching you and your young children struggle to make it on your own.

Your family and friends also have a hard time seeing you unhappy. Most likely, they equate your happiness with having a new man around. With the best of intentions, they think another man will mend your broken heart. When you take an interest in other men and start to date again, they feel you are getting on with your life. We are not exactly sure, though, what "getting on with your life" means. It is one of those "dumb things people say"—another morsel of unsolicited advice freely given to widows.

★ ★ ★

Lesson Learned

Our society likes couples, especially young and happy ones.

TIMING

It is assumed you'll date again, so the question becomes not "if" but "when." The world usually expects you to wait one year before you get involved with a new man. That's the old standard for a widow's mourning period.

Sometimes, widows get mixed messages from family and friends about dating. On the one hand, people may urge you to move forward with your life. On the other hand, if you date too soon, you may be criticized for not respecting your late husband's memory, not loving him enough, or some other reason related to your moral character. As with most things in life, you can't please everyone.

More importantly, what the world often fails to consider is when you are ready to date. Dating after widowhood is a lot like jumping into the ocean. Some women run up to the surf and dive head-on into the first wave. Others test out the waters by sticking their toes into the surf and getting wet little by little. There is less risk when you gradually get wet but more adventure when you jump right in. In the end, everyone ends up in the ocean. It's the same with dating. Whether you're swimming in the ocean, or back in the dating world, be sure to watch out for sharks.

★ ★ ★

Echo
"After my first date I went home, looked at my husband's picture, and yelled at him for dying on me."

There is no right or wrong time for you to date again, although you need to be honest with yourself and be certain you aren't looking for a relationship with another man to avoid grieving for your husband. Remember, when you avoid grief, it will come back when you least expect it. You should heal emotionally before you get romantically involved again.

Some widows go out on their first date just a few months after their husband's death. It takes others a year or two to accept that he is dead, much less to think about another man or relationship. Your readiness to date will depend on your relationship with your husband, the circumstances of his death, and how you're coping with the complexities of military widowhood.

We think it is important to understand yourself a little more before you get involved with another man. Giving some thought to your reasons for dating will help you understand yourself, and your needs, a little better. Read this list of questions and spend a few moments mulling over your answers.

- Are you emotionally ready to let a new man into your life?
- Are you dating because your mother, family, or friends are urging you to do it?
- Is loneliness driving you into the dating world?
- Are you tired of being the only woman without a man?
- Do you miss male companionship, attention, affection, and sex?
- Are you in need of a handyman around your house?
- Do you long to be wanted or needed?
- Are you looking to replace your husband?
- Are you searching for a father for your children?
- Do you want someone to support you financially?

Consider your answers carefully. Wanting a handyman around the house does not mean you are ready for a new relationship.

Your First Relationship

It is especially hard to get involved with another man when you are still in love with your husband. One of the tasks of widowhood is to convert your feelings of being *in love* with your husband to feelings *of love* for him. Death did not make you stop loving your husband, and it's okay to still feel love. To be *in love* with someone, however, requires an ongoing relationship. This cannot happen, no matter how much you want it.

Your first relationship will likely be tumultuous. It will include you, the new man in your life, and the memory of your late husband. It can get a bit crowded. While you may want to tell this new man everything about yourself, resist the urge to share every last detail. He probably does not want to hear about the fabulous long weekend you and your husband spent in London, or the details of your wedding.

★ ★ ★
Lesson Learned
You have to let go of an old relationship in order to make room for a new one.

You can and will find love again, but it will be a different love from the one you shared with your husband. That's just the way it is. Don't rush into making another commitment just because a new man makes you feel alive again. Take your time and get to know him. Make sure he is right for you.

MILITARY MEN

If you decide to date military men, just about everyone you know will have an opinion—and they will offer it to you without the slightest hesitation. People have strong personal views on this subject, so if you do date military men, be prepared for some unsolicited feedback.

Likewise, widows also have some strong opinions about dating military men. Some widows want nothing to do with the military. They don't like the lifestyle and want their next relationship to be with someone in a different line of work. Other widows are afraid to tempt fate, fearing the worst will happen again. On the flip side, some widows are more comfortable in the military world than in civilian life. They like the kind of men who join the military, and they see the lifestyle as an adventure rather than a burden. These women do not fear that lightning will strike twice.

★ ★ ★

Lesson Learned

Follow your heart and use your head when you date again.

FOUR SCENARIOS OF DATING

Having been there, done that, and gotten the T-shirt, there is no need for you to reinvent the wheel when it comes to figuring out men. Here are some dating scenarios you will encounter:

- Right man, right time. It's a lot like hitting the jackpot on a slot machine. The lights flash, the bells and whistles go off, and you get the big payoff. Just when you're ready for a relationship, Mr. Right comes along.
- Right man, wrong time. You meet the next Mr. Right, but the timing is all wrong. This situation can be tricky, but not impossible. You will need to understand why it's not the right time, and figure out if it's worth hanging in there.
- Wrong man, right time. Danger . . . red alert!!! You may be ready for a relationship, but he is Mr. Wrong. You can't change

him, so run—fast—before you invest any time or emotional energy and risk getting hurt. The wrong man does not get better with time.

• Wrong man, wrong time. Don't waste your time or tempt fate. If he is Mr. Wrong now, he will not transform into Mr. Right later.

★ ★ ★

Lesson Learned

It is possible to fall in love with the wrong man, so be careful.

Putting It All Together

Our lighthearted advice: dating is like playing the instant lottery. You buy a ticket, rub off the numbers, and instantly know if you have a winner or a loser. Sometimes you are pleasantly surprised when you win a small prize, a few dollars, or another ticket. However, you know up front if this ticket is the big winner. If your ticket isn't a winner now, it isn't going to turn into a winner later. No matter how hard you try, you can't change it into a bigger or better prize. The smart thing to do is to go buy another ticket and try your luck again.

This same advice applies to dating. There are many good men out there. Make sure you have a winner. You deserve to be happy again. Don't settle for less just to be in a relationship or to get married again.

CHAPTER 29

★ ★ ★

GROWTH AFTER LOSS

Antoine and Vanessa

Vanessa, fifty-three, lost her husband, Antoine, in the First Gulf War in 1991. A gunnery sergeant in the Marine Corps, he was killed in a firefight in Kuwait in the early days of Operation Desert Storm. Although it was many years ago, Vanessa still has an emptiness in her heart when she thinks of Antoine.

After Antoine's death, Vanessa moved back home to Bayside, New York, not far from Shea Stadium, the home of the New York Mets. They were Antoine's favorite team when he was growing up, and whenever the family was back in Queens, they went to as many games as they could. Even now, it is bittersweet when Vanessa passes the stadium on the subway.

Surrounded by her family and friends, Vanessa came back to life as she worked through her grief. She took a job in the registrar's office at the local community college. As time passed, she wanted to do something more challenging. She talked to a guidance counselor in the adult education office and realized she wanted to become a registered nurse.

It was a long and hard struggle, but her family—especially her two children—were very supportive. In a reversal of roles, the kids taught her how to do online research and helped her to write term papers.

Vanessa loved her clinical nursing courses, especially when she worked with critically ill patients. The patients told her she

was easy to talk to. Vanessa felt she was helping them emotionally as well as physically. She believes her own experience as a
young military widow prepared her to help others going
through difficult times.

Vanessa never thought she'd see the day when she received
her bachelor's degree in nursing. She then passed her nursing
boards with flying colors. Now she works in a large cancer center in New York City. After she gets some experience, Vanessa
wants to get her master's degree.

*t*HERE IS NO WAY YOU CAN REMAIN the same person you were before
your husband died; death has a way of changing those who are left behind.
It may be hard for you to imagine that anything good can come out of your
husband's death. It is likely, however, that over time, you will see positive
changes within yourself. These changes may not become obvious until you
have worked through a good deal of your grief.

Earlier in this book, we talked about how people who have experienced trauma and loss search to understand why traumatic things
happened to them and their loved ones. This is often a long and difficult
process. In fact, your search may continue and change as the years progress.

At first, you may feel that your husband's death has only negative
effects on your mind, body, and spirit. For a long time, it seems that
nothing good can come out of it. But research shows that people can
grow, or even be transformed, in the face of overwhelming psychological pain. This growth is not something another person can or should
impose upon you, however.

POTENTIAL AREAS OF GROWTH

In a review of previous studies, Tedeschi and Calhoun (1995) found
that people who have experienced psychological trauma report three areas
of benefit: positive changes in themselves, positive changes in relationships
with others, and a positive change in their philosophy of life.

POSITIVE CHANGES IN THEMSELVES

The first positive change was a sense of emotional growth. A part of this
growth was an increased feeling of self-reliance, or the ability to handle

other difficult events or situations. Not everyone who reported this change found they were successful in coping with the trauma when it first happened, because they were not prepared for it. This change showed up later, as they coped with other problems that resulted from the original trauma. As your life moves forward you, too, might feel more assertive and confident about dealing with future difficulties.

★　★　★
Echo
"My husband's death was the hardest thing I've ever had to deal with. If I can handle that, I can handle anything."

Another positive change was a new awareness of vulnerability. That might not sound like a good thing at first, but the people in the study came to understand that they are not immortal. Bad things can happen to good people. When overwhelming events occur in your life, you need others.

POSITIVE CHANGES IN RELATIONSHIPS WITH OTHERS
The second perceived benefit of growth after loss and trauma, and the realization of how fragile their lives were, was a desire to strengthen relationships with loved ones. Tedeschi and Calhoun reported that some people who experienced loss later found it easier to more openly express their emotions. Through trial and error, these individuals found people who were willing to listen to them.

Some people found that this new comfort in expressing their feelings, combined with a new understanding of their vulnerability, made them more compassionate toward others. This gave them a greater capacity to understand and accept what other people were going through.

When you are more open, it is easier to share your experiences and coping strategies with others going through similar circumstances. Being a resource can boost your feelings of competence and self-esteem.

A POSITIVE CHANGE IN THEIR PHILOSOPHY OF LIFE
While coming to grips with the pain and suffering associated with traumatic loss, some people reported a different understanding of, and appreciation for, their own lives. The ongoing search for meaning in your new life may lead you to change your priorities. You may realize that you

should make the best use of your time here on earth. Wolfelt (2003) viewed this search for meaning as a challenge to become your best self.

THINGS THAT WILL PROMOTE POSITIVE OUTCOMES

Tedeschi and Calhoun further explored a number of guideposts for people who were dealing with traumatic experiences. Some of them have already been discussed in this book; namely, helping others and letting them help you, using humor to cope with difficult situations, and considering the spiritual issues that arise when an overwhelming experience pulls the rug out from under you.

In *Trauma and Transformation: Growing in the Aftermath of Suffering* (1995), the authors also recommend the following:
- Learn from your experiences. These lessons are hard won.
- Change your thinking. You are dealing with a "survivable challenge."
- Seek out books on surviving crises and trauma. Learn from other people's experiences.
- Actively look for positive changes in yourself. You might not have noticed them.

Wolfelt (2003) similarly talked about the importance of nourishing yourself by focusing on what gives your life meaning and purpose, giving back to others, and paying attention to your own needs.

★ ★ ★
Lesson Learned
Even the worst trauma can produce positive changes in you.

PUTTING IT ALL TOGETHER

The process of personal change that you have undergone since your husband died is a difficult one, full of stops and starts. It is hard to imagine that anything good can come of such a painful loss.

Remember that no one else can tell you that you *will* or *should* experience emotional or spiritual growth. But if you do begin to see positive changes in yourself, it is definitely a good thing. Stand by; there are more good changes to come.

CHAPTER 30

★ ★ ★

IN CASE OF EMERGENCY

Scott and Stacy

Scott, forty-one, was a senior chief in the Coast Guard, stationed in Alaska. He lived with his wife, Stacy, and their three children in Eagle River, a town ten miles north of Anchorage. Scott and Stacy had their share of ups and downs during their nineteen years of marriage. Like many military families, however, they felt that duty in Alaska was good for them as a couple, and as a family, bringing them closer together. This was their second tour in the state, and they liked it so much, they wanted to open a bed and breakfast there when Scott retired.

In early July, Scott flew out to investigate an accidental death on a commercial fishing vessel in Bristol Bay. On the final approach of the commercial flight from Dillingham to Egegik, the pilot lost control of the aircraft in the turbulence coming off the bay. The plane crash-landed in the Naknek River, just a few hundred yards from the runway. Neither Scott's body nor those of the other five passengers were found because of the glacial runoff, which made the river murky.

Scott was the one in the marriage who paid all the bills. Now that Stacy had to figure out how he had managed their money, she wished he had involved her more in their finances. Scott wasn't too organized when it came to keeping records or important papers together. Stacy was overwhelmed by the sheer number of financial and legal documents she needed after her husband's death. She was angry with him for not keeping everything in one place.

After this ordeal, Stacy realized she needed to put her own affairs in order, so that all of her important data was organized and accessible, should the unthinkable happen to her. She compiled this information into one document and put it in a sealed envelope. She gave the envelope to her sister with the following instructions written on it: "To Be Opened in the Event of My Death or Grave Illness."

Her oldest son, who was eighteen, had already reported to the Coast Guard Academy in New London, Connecticut, to follow in his father's footsteps. Preparing for the worst, Stacy needed to decide who would be the legal guardians for her younger children. After talking with them, Stacy named her sister and brother-in-law as guardians, just in case. It was hard to face these issues, but it gave Stacy great peace of mind knowing her children would be properly cared for.

*a*FTER YOUR EXPERIENCE WITH your husband's death, you know what a hassle it was to search for legal documents, financial statements, and important military paperwork. If you were like many couples, you and your husband did not keep this information in an easily accessible place; you stuffed it in a variety of files, envelopes, and boxes. There was a good chance it wasn't well organized; you probably moved it a few times when you transferred to new duty stations. Perhaps after each move you thought that you should organize all this stuff—some day.

We have not included this chapter to add another item to your already long "To-Do" list. With what you have been through, however, you now realize that bad things can happen to good people, and they happen swiftly.

In the event you die or are incapacitated, you want the best decisions made for your medical care. You also want your children to be taken care of legally, emotionally, and financially. Now that you are widowed, it is especially important to organize your personal affairs and important papers; you are the only one who knows where this information is located. To ensure this process goes as smoothly as possible in the event something happens to you, you'll have to do some advance planning. As you found out firsthand, being organized is important. You don't want your family or friends to be forced to sort through your personal files, looking for the documents they need.

Planning for the future and imposing order on your important papers is not something you can do in one sitting—but it is certainly worth the time and energy you put into it. Now is the time to start.

★   ★   ★

Lesson Learned
*It is essential to plan for your children's security and the
execution of your last wishes.*

We have provided some guidelines that will help you in this process, and we suggest you adapt this information to meet your specific personal and family needs.

IMPORTANT DECISIONS

First of all, you have some important and sobering decisions to make. Don't make them casually or without guidance. Your safety and welfare, and that of your children, may depend on them. Talk with trusted family members or your clergyman. Consult with a financial adviser. Get legal advice from an attorney.

LEGAL GUARDIANSHIP OF YOUR CHILDREN

Decide who will raise your kids if you should die. Be sure to discuss this issue with your children, as well as the individual(s) you would like to designate as their guardians.

LAST WILL AND TESTAMENT

You need to make out a new will after your husband's death. You must decide whom you will name as the executor of your estate. Think about how you want your monetary and sentimental possessions distributed. Include any specific bequests to your children, other family members, or friends. You may also want to set up a trust for your children.

HEALTH–CARE ISSUES

You have several important decisions to make concerning your health care in the event you become incapacitated or unable to make your own decisions. First, you should decide now, while you are healthy, what instructions you want followed in the event you are unable to make your wishes known. This information usually includes what health-care measures you do and do not want taken. You also have an opportunity to specify what comfort measures you want administered. The term "living will" is often used to describe this information, although its definition differs from state to state.

Next, designate someone to act on your behalf (a health-care proxy) to make sure your wishes are carried out. Discuss your wishes with this person so he or she clearly understands your feelings regarding extraordinary medical measures. The health-care proxy form is sometimes called a "Durable Power of Attorney for Health Care."

In many states, an advance health-care directive will include both the living will and the health-care proxy. Your physician should be able to provide you with a copy of this form or tell you how to get one. Appendix B includes some Web sites you can search to get information on the forms used in your state.

You may already have filled out copies of health-care proxy or advance health-care directive forms in another state. If you move to a new state, however, be sure to check that the forms you signed include the information required by your new state. There may also be a difference in states' requirements on how the forms are witnessed and if they must be notarized.

Give copies of your completed forms to your family doctor and the person you named as your health-care proxy. Place copies of these forms in your medical chart. Keep a copy with your other important documents.

STORING THIS INFORMATION

We suggest you keep all these documents together in a clearly marked file. It is a good idea to invest in a fireproof box and keep them in it. You might also consider storing these items in a safe-deposit box at your local bank. We also suggest you give a master list of essential information to a family member or friend or tell them where it is located.

MASTER LIST INFORMATION

Here are suggestions for the types of documents and information that should be included on your master list. Your list may not look exactly like this one. Include anything you think will be helpful.

PERSONAL DATA

- Your full legal name and SSN; include your maiden name
- Your husband's full name and SSN
- Your children's full names and SSNs

IMPORTANT DOCUMENTS

- Last will and testament
- Power of attorney
- Health-care proxy
- Advance health-care directive
- Birth certificates
- Adoption papers
- Marriage certificate
- Your husband's death certificate
- Your husband's DD1300—Report of Casualty
- Your husband's DD214—Certificate of Release or Discharge from active duty
- Separation and divorce agreements
- VA Certificate of Eligibility
- Passport(s)
- Tax records
- Mortgage documents
- Property deeds
- Alarm system codes
- Car titles
- Insurance policies
- Stock certificates and savings bonds
- Financial statements
- Medical and dental records

PROPERTY INFORMATION

- Property address
- Company holding mortgage or lease
- Account number

INSURANCE

- Insurance company
- Address
- Account number
- Type of insurance: life, car, homeowner, rental, or personal articles

FINANCIAL

- Bank or credit union
    Address
    Account numbers
    Type of account: checking, savings, loans
    Safe-deposit box information and location of key
    Online passwords
- Credit card(s)
    Type of card
    Issuing financial institution
    Card number
- Financial adviser (including address and phone number)
- Accountant (including address and phone number)

LEGAL

- Attorney (including address and phone number)

COMPUTER

- Account passwords
- ISP passwords

MEDICAL

- Type of medical coverage (primary and secondary)
- Provider and policy number
- Primary care physician (including address and phone number)
- Dentist (including address and phone number)
- Other medical specialists (pediatrician, allergist, psychiatrist, therapist, including addresses and phone numbers)

RELIGIOUS AFFILIATION

- Church/synagogue/mosque/house of worship
- Pastor, rabbi, or religious leader (including address and phone number)

EMPLOYER

- Company name
- Immediate supervisor (including address and phone number)

NEXT OF KIN

- Name (including address and phone number)
- Relationship

NEIGHBORS

- Names (including address and phone number)

CLOSE FRIENDS

- Names (including address and phone number)

We know this is tough stuff, but it is also very important. Once you have assembled this master list, make several copies. Keep one copy in your fireproof box with all your other important documents. Put another copy in a sealed envelope and give it to a trusted loved one or the executor of your estate, along with instructions to open it in case you are gravely ill or have died.

★   ★   ★

Lesson Learned
Be prepared for the worst and hope for the best.

PUTTING IT ALL TOGETHER

No one likes to deal with these details. Taking these measures, however, is realistic and practical. It will help to ensure that your wishes are known and your children will be taken care of, should the worst happen. Having your affairs in order will not ease the emotional burden on those you leave behind, but it will make it easier for them to tend to your personal affairs.

Now that you have planned for the worst, it's time to start enjoying life again!

APPENDIX A

★ ★ ★

HOW YOU CAN HELP THE MILITARY WIDOW

THIS SECTION IS FOR YOU IF:
- your command has experienced a death, and you want to provide the right support to the surviving spouse;
- you are assigned as a casualty officer to a new widow; or
- someone you know became a military widow.

We know you want to help, or you wouldn't be reading this book. Like most people, however, you probably don't know what to say or do, or you are afraid of doing the wrong thing.

HOW COMMAND PERSONNEL CAN HELP THE MILITARY WIDOW

Here are some suggestions for ways in which you and your command can help the military widow.

INITIAL ASSISTANCE
- Treat her as you would like your own wife to be treated if she were in this position.
- Don't try to protect her from information about her husband's death. If she is asking questions, she is ready for answers. She may not like what you are telling her, but she does want to know.
- Never use the phrase, "I can't tell you." Even if your reasons are valid, she won't hear them. She will think you're hiding something from her. Instead, say, "I can't answer that question right now."

- "I don't know" is an honest answer. Don't speculate or repeat rumors.
- Never use the word "closure." It does not exist.
- If she prefers not to talk with the media, have the PAO handle them for her.
- Shock and grief can significantly slow down a widow's ability to make sense of what you are telling her. You may have to repeat information several times before she understands it. Be patient.
- Bereaved people may behave in ways that make no sense to you. Grief reactions are not logical or rational. Again, be patient and nonjudgmental.
- Don't assume she knows how the military works. Let her know what to expect and when. The military culture may be especially confusing to National Guard or Reserve widows, who have limited exposure to it.
- If her husband died on deployment or at sea, ask her if she wants his clothes washed or returned *as is*. She may want his belongings to smell like him rather than laundry detergent.
- Don't help out at her house without asking first. That squeaky door may remind her of her husband.
- Don't assume you know what she needs. Ask her.
- Include the military family support group in assisting her and her family. They can help with meals, child care, and refreshments for the funeral or memorial service.

FUNERAL AND MEMORIAL SERVICES

- Remember, you are helping to bury a fallen comrade or shipmate.
- If she decides on a military funeral for her husband, offer to let her personalize it. The same thing goes for the memorial service.
- If she is not familiar with the rituals and traditions of a military funeral or memorial service, tell her what to expect so she won't be blindsided. This may be especially important if she doesn't know about the rifle salute, the Final Roll Call, or the Missing Man flyby. She may not know she can obtain mementos from the service, such as the spent shells from the rifle salute.

- Be sensitive to how her husband died. For example, if he was killed by gunfire, she may not want the rifle salute at his funeral.
- Allow her and her family to see ahead of time where the service will be held.
- Offer to pick up out-of-town relatives at the airport. Assist them with hotel and car rental arrangements, as well as base or post access and directions.
- Find out how many family members will be attending and reserve enough chairs or pews for them. Have tissues available in the seating area.
- Offer to videotape the funeral and the memorial services, especially if the widow has children.
- Have a guest book or scrapbook available so friends and visitors can share memories of her husband. Consider having a video camera at the funeral or memorial reception and encourage people to share stories about him.

ONGOING HELP

- Make sure she has the correct contact numbers for ongoing needs, such as benefits and counseling.
- Ask her if she wants someone to explain the accident report or autopsy results: they may contain graphic or disturbing information.
- Tell her when the accident report will be released to the media. It may be carried as a news story.
- Wherever possible, don't let her find out about developments in the investigation of her husband's death from news reports.

How Family Members and Friends Can Help the Military Widow

- If she is not having a military funeral for her husband, offer to help with the private funeral arrangements. This is probably the first time she has had to plan a funeral, and it may be overwhelming.
- Ask what you can do to help. You can assist with small matters, like washing clothes, or big tasks, like making a picture collage for the service.

- Offer to help her write thank-you notes after the funeral.
- Don't avoid her because you don't know what to say. Sometimes, just your supportive presence is enough.
- Use her husband's name when talking about him. People think using his name will upset her. It won't.
- Be prepared for a wide range of feelings and reactions for a long time.
- Don't judge her behaviors. She is doing the best she can, given the circumstances.
- Bring meals and nourishing snacks to have on hand. Comfort food is always welcome.
- Help her return the empty casserole dishes.
- Be a good listener.
- Laugh with her. Share funny stories about her husband. She will love to hear these, especially stories she hasn't heard before.
- Watch the kids so she can have some time to herself.
- Help her sort through her husband's clothes, when she is ready.
- Call her on significant dates, such as the anniversary of his death. It will make her feel good to know that her husband is remembered.
- Seek out and suggest local support groups she can attend. Offer to go to the first meeting with her. It will help her feel more comfortable.
- Offer to take her to visit her husband's grave the first time. Going alone may be more than she can handle.
- During the holidays, remember this new widow. Don't ignore the fact that there will be an empty chair at her table.
- Ask her if she wants to attend Memorial Day or Veterans Day ceremonies.
- Make a donation in her husband's name to her favorite charity. Check with her first, though.

APPENDIX B

★ ★ ★

RESOURCES

HEALTH AND ILLNESS

American Cancer Society
    Phone: 800-ACS-2345 (227-2345)
    Web address: http://www.americancancersociety.org

American Heart Association
    7272 Greenville Avenue
    Dallas, TX 75231
    Phone: 800-AHA-USA1 (242-8721)
    Web address: http://www.americanheart.org

American Stroke Association
    7272 Greenville Avenue
    Dallas, TX 75231
    Phone: 888-4-STROKE (478-7653)
    Web address: http://www.strokeassociation.org

HOSPICELINE—Hospice Education Institute
    3 Unity Square
    P.O. Box 98
    Machiasport, ME 04655
    Phone: 800-331-1620
    E-mail address: hospiceall@aol.com
    Web address: http://www.hospiceworld.org

Provides information on hospice services, as well as referrals to local agencies. Many community hospices provide bereavement services whether or not your husband was under their care when he died.

U.S. Department of Agriculture (USDA)
Web address: http://www.MyPyramid.gov

Latest information for children and adults on the "food pyramid."

VICTIMS OF CRIME

Federal Trade Commission (FTC)
Web address: http://www.consumer.gov/idtheft/ or http://www.ftc.gov/bcp/conline/pubs/credit/_idtheft.htm

Provides resources on a wide range of topics on preventing and dealing with identity theft.

Mothers Against Drunk Driving (MADD)
511 East John Carpenter Freeway, Suite 700
Irving, TX 75062
Phone: 800-GET-MADD (438-6233)
Web address: http://www.madd.org

National Association of Crime Victim Compensation Boards
Web address: http://www.nacvcb.org

Provides links to state crime victim compensation boards. Compensation covers a wide range of costs incurred as a result of criminal victimization, including counseling for families of murder victims. Compensation and requirements vary widely according to state.

National Center for Victims of Crime (NCVC)
2000 M Street, NW, Suite 480
Washington, D.C. 20036
Phone: 800-FYI-CALL (394-2255)

Fax: 202-467-8701

TTY: 800-211-7996

E-mail address: gethelp@ncvc.org

Web address: http://www.ncvc.org

Click on "Get Help Series," then click on specific topics: "Homicide Survivors," "PTSD," "Grief: Children," "Acquaintance Rape," "Rape-Related PTSD," and "Identity Theft." Also provides information on local referrals, current projects, and useful information for crime victims.

National Organization for Victim Assistance (NOVA)

510 King Street, Suite 424

Alexandria, VA 22314

Phone: 703-535-NOVA (6682) or 800-879-NOVA (6682)

Fax: 703-535-5500

Web address: http://www.trynova.org

Provides information and nationwide referrals to victims of violent crimes. Also coordinates national crisis response teams following disasters or acts of terrorism.

The National Women's Health Information Center

Phone: 800-994-9662

Web addresses: http://www.womenshealth.gov or http://www.4woman.gov/faq/rohypnol.htm

For more information on date rape drugs and how you can protect yourself from becoming a victim of sexual assault. Call if you don't have Web access and they will send information in the mail.

Parents of Murdered Children (POMC)

100 East Eighth Street, Suite B-41

Cincinnati, OH 45202

Phone: 888-818-POMC (7662)

E-mail address: natlpomc@aol.com

Web address: http://www.pomc.org

For the families and friends of those who have died by violence.

MILITARY LOSS

Gold Star Wives
   Web address: http://www.goldstarwives.org

Military One Source
   Web address: http://www.militaryonesource.com

Society of Military Widows
   Phone: 800-842-3451, ext. 3009
   Web address: http://www.militarywidows.org

Tragedy Assistance Program for Survivors, Inc. (TAPS)
   1621 Connecticut Avenue, NW, Suite 300
   Washington, D.C. 20009
   Phone: 202-588-TAPS (8277)
   Hotline: 800-959-TAPS (8277)
   E-mail address: info@taps.org
   Web address: http://www.taps.org

   Holds an annual conference over Memorial Day weekend in
   Washington, D.C., for loved ones grieving the loss of someone in
   the military. See also information under "Grieving Children."

U.S. Department of Veterans Affairs—Readjustment Counseling Service
   Phone: 202-273-9116
   Web addresses: http://www.va.gov or http://www.va.gov/rcs

   Provides in-person and phone bereavement counseling services
   for widows, parents, siblings, and children of deceased servicemen
   and women in all fifty states plus Puerto Rico, Guam, and the U.S.
   Virgin Islands. Also provides local community referrals and information about application for benefits. No time limit for bereavement services.

United Warrior Survivor Foundation (UWSF)
   P. O. Box 181097
   Coronado, CA 92178
   Phone: 877-804-UWSF (8973)

Fax: 413-677-1143

Web address: http://www.FrogFriends.com

Committed to assisting the surviving spouses of special operations personnel who have been killed in the line of duty since September 11, 2001. Offers a range of services and programs for surviving spouses and their children.

SUICIDE PREVENTION

If you or someone you know is in danger of committing suicide, immediately call 800-273-TALK (8255) or dial 911.

American Association of Suicidology
Web address: http://www.suicidology.org

Center for Disease Control (CDC)
Web address: http://www.cdc.gov

National Institute of Mental Health (NIMH)
Web address: http://www.nimh.nih.gov

National Mental Health Association (NMHA)
Web address: http://www.nmha.org
Site also has links to state mental health associations.

National Strategy for Suicide Prevention
Web address: http://www.mentalhealth.samhsa.gov

GRIEF AND BEREAVEMENT

American Association of Retired Persons (AARP)
Web address: http://www.aarp.org/life/griefandloss/
Provides information about normal reactions to loss for older and younger widows. Also includes practical information for planning funerals, handling financial issues, and claiming benefits.

Young Widows or Widowers (YWOW)
P.O. Box 6525
Virginia Beach, VA 23456
Phone: 866-876-YWOW (9969) or 757-468-2144
Fax: 757-368-9174
E-mail address: info@ywow.org
Web address: http://www.ywow.org

COUNSELING REFERRALS

Association for Death Education and Counseling (ADEC)
60 Revere Drive, Suite 500
Northbrook, IL 60062
Phone: 847-509-0403
Fax: 847-480-9282
E-mail address: adec@adec.org
Web address: http://www.adec.org

Click on "Human Resources Network" and then on your state to obtain a list of members in your area who can answer questions or provide local counseling resources.

International Society for Traumatic Stress Studies (ISTSS)
60 Revere Drive, Suite 500
Northbrook, IL 60062
Phone: 847-480-9028
Fax: 847-480-9282
E-mail address: istss@istss.org
Web address: http://www.istss.org

Log on to http://www.istss.org/terrorism/sudden_traumatic_loss.htm for information on trauma, loss, and traumatic grief.

GRIEVING CHILDREN

Comfort Zone Camp
  2101-A Westmoreland Street
  Richmond, VA 23230
  Phone: 866-488-5679 or 804-377-3430
  Fax: 804-377-3433
  Web address: http://www.comfortzonecamp.org

  Several times a year runs grief camps for children ages seven to twelve and thirteen to seventeen. Camps are usually in the Richmond, Virginia, area. No cost to attend and some travel scholarships available.

The Dougy Center for Grieving Children and Families
  P.O. Box 86852
  Portland, OR 97286
  Phone: 866-775-5683 or 503-775-5683
  Fax: 503-777-3097
  E-mail address: help@dougy.org
  Web address: http://www.dougy.org

  Provides information on grieving and activities that can help children and teenagers cope with their grief. Also has information on ordering books for children coping with the death of a parent, as well as workbooks for children dealing with suicide and murder.

Tragedy Assistance Program for Survivors, Inc. (TAPS)
  1621 Connecticut Avenue, NW, Suite 300
  Washington, D.C. 20009
  Phone: 202-588-TAPS (8277)
  Hotline: 800-959-TAPS (8277)
  E-mail address: info@taps.org
  Web address: http://www.taps.org

  In conjunction with the annual Memorial Day conference (see description under "Military Loss"), TAPS also holds "Good Grief Camp for Young Survivors."

BENEFITS

U.S. Department of Defense—TRICARE
Web address: http://www.tricare.osd.mil/factsheets

Obtain fact sheets entitled, "How TRICARE Changes When a Military Sponsor Dies or Retires" and "TRICARE Dental Program Survivor Benefits."

U.S. Department of Veterans Affairs—Beneficiary Financial Counseling
Web address: Go to http://www.va.gov, then click on "Benefits," then "Survivor Benefits," then "Death in Service," and then "VA Benefits and Services." Scroll down to "Life Insurance" or try http://www.vba.va.gov/survivors/VAbenefits.htm.

CASUALTY ASSISTANCE HEADQUARTERS

U.S. Air Force
Casualty Matters Division
Headquarters Air Force Personnel Center
550 C Street West, Suite 14
Randolph Air Force Base, TX 78150
Phone: 800-433-0048
Web address: http://www.afpc.randolph.af.mil/casualty/

U.S. Army
Casualty and Memorial Affairs Operations Center
U.S. Army Human Resources Command
200 Stovall Street
Alexandria, VA 22332-0470
Phone: 800-626-3317

Web address: Go to https://www.hrc.army.mil/indexflash.asp, then click on "Alexandria," then "Soldier, Family and Retiree/Veteran Information," and then "Casualty and Funerals."

U.S. Coast Guard
Commandant (CG-1222)
U.S. Coast Guard
2100 Second Street, SW
Washington, D.C. 20593
E-mail address: compensation@comdt.uscg.mil

U.S. Marine Corps
Headquarters U.S. Marine Corps
Manpower and Reserve Affairs
ATTN: MRPC
3280 Russell Road
Quantico, VA 22134
Phone: 800-847-1597

Web address: Go to https://www.manpower.usmc.mil, scroll to "Top Requests," then click on "Casualty Assistance."

U.S. Navy
Navy Personnel Command (PERS-62)
5720 Integrity Drive
Millington, TN 38055-6200
Phone: 800-368-3202
Web address:
http://www.npc.navy.mil/CommandSupport/CasualtyAssistance/

IN CASE OF EMERGENCY

Aging with Dignity
Web address: http://www.agingwithdignity.org

Provides information on the "Five Wishes," an easy-to-use legal document that can assist you in planning for your medical care in the event you are incapacitated or unable to make your own medical decisions.

American Association for Retired Persons (AARP)
> Web address: http://www.aarp.org

> For information and a checklist on handling final details and getting your affairs in order.

U.S. Living Will Registry
> Web address: http://www.uslivingwillregistry.com

> Provides information on what kinds of issues need to be considered in completing the advance health-care directive, how to choose a health-care proxy, specific information for each state regarding requirements and forms, a link to legal assistance in your area, and information on how to register your advance health-care directive so that it is accessible and available to health-care professionals twenty-four hours a day.

REFERENCES

Cousins, Norman. 1979. *Anatomy of an Illness as Perceived by the Patient.* New York: W. W. Norton.

Doka, Kenneth J. 2002. "Introduction." In *Disenfranchised Grief: New Directions, Challenges and Strategies for Practice,* ed. Kenneth J. Doka, 5–22. Champaign, Ill.: Research Press.

Federal Trade Commission. "Identity Theft." http://www.consumer.gov/idtheft (accessed June 27, 2005).

Holmes, T. H., and R. H. Rahe. 1967. "The Social Readjustment Scale." *Journal of Psychosomatic Research* 11:213–18.

How Stuff Works. "How Laughter Works." http://www.howstuffworks.com (accessed April 25, 2005).

Kübler-Ross, Elisabeth. 1969. *On Death and Dying.* New York: Macmillan Publishing Co.

Kushner, Harold S. 1981. *When Bad Things Happen to Good People.* New York: Avon Books.

McGhee, Paul E. 1998. "Humor and Health." http://www.holisticonline.com/Humor_Therapy/humor_mcghee_article.htm (accessed April 4, 2005).

McKinley Health Center, University of Illinois at Urbana Champaign. "Date Rape Drugs—What You Need to Know About Them." http://www.mckinley.uiuc.edu/handouts/date_rape_drugs.html (accessed February 6, 2006).

National Mental Health Association. "Suicide Fact Sheet."
http://www.nmha.org (accessed May 6, 2005).

Rando, Therese A. 1993. *Treatment of Complicated Mourning.*
Champaign, Ill.: Research Press.

Read-Brown, Ken. "Norman Cousins: Editor and Writer: 1915–1990."
http://www.harvardsquarelibrary.org/unitarians/cousins.html
(accessed August 18, 2005).

Reed, M. D., and J. Y. Greenwald. 1991. "Survivor-Victim Status,
Attachment, and Sudden Death." *Suicide and Life-Threatening
Behavior* 21:385–400.

Schiraldi, Glenn R. 2000. *The Post-Traumatic Stress Disorder Sourcebook.*
Los Angeles, Calif.: Lowell House.

Shear, M. C., A. Zuckoff, and E. Frank. 2001. "The Syndrome of
Traumatic Grief." *CNS Spectrums* 6:339–46.

Skorucak, Anton. 2002. "The Science of Tears." http://www.scienceiq.com/
(accessed September 27, 2005).

Tedeschi, Richard G., and Lawrence G. Calhoun. 1995. *Trauma and
Transformation: Growing in the Aftermath of Suffering.* Thousand Oaks,
Calif.: Sage Publications.

U.S. Department of Defense, Washington Headquarters Services,
Directorate for Information Operations and Reports. "U.S. Active
Duty Military Deaths per 100,000 Serving—1980 through 2004."
http://www.dior.whs.mil/mmid/casualty/Death_Rates.pdf (accessed
February 6, 2006).

Wolfelt, Alan D. 1992. *Understanding Grief: Helping Yourself Heal.* Muncie,
Ind.: Accelerated Development.

———. 1993. "Identification of 'Grief Avoidance Response Patterns': A
Growing Phenomenon." *The Forum Newsletter* (Association for Death
Education and Counseling) XVIII (January–February): 16–19.

————. 2000. *Healing Your Grieving Heart: 100 Practical Ideas for Kids.* Ft. Collins, Colo.: Companion Press.

————. 2003. *Understanding Your Grief: Ten Essential Touchstones for Finding Hope and Healing Your Heart.* Ft. Collins, Colo.: Companion Press.

ABOUT THE AUTHORS

JOANNE STEEN, MS, NCC, is the widow of a naval aviator who was killed in the line of duty. An engineer turned nationally certified counselor who specializes in traumatic grief and crisis response, she is also a certified strategic planner, grief group founder, crisis responder, instructor, and speaker on military loss. For her work with the Department of the Navy, Joanne was awarded the Meritorious Civilian Service Medal.

M. REGINA ASARO, MS, RN, CT, completed her nursing education over the course of eleven moves as a military wife. Regina has worked in in-patient psychiatric units at the National Institutes of Health and at Gorgas Army Hospital in Panama. She has also served as director of crime victim assistance programs for victims of sexual assault and families of murder victims. As a crisis responder, Regina has worked on teams that responded to the bombing in Oklahoma City, the crash of Flight KAL801 on Guam, and in Tuzla, Bosnia, following the massacre of civilians in Srebrenica. She has presented many workshops on the impact of violent crime, grief, and traumatic loss.

THE NAVAL INSTITUTE PRESS is the book-publishing arm of the U.S. Naval Institute, a private, nonprofit, membership society for sea service professionals and others who share an interest in naval and maritime affairs. Established in 1873 at the U.S. Naval Academy in Annapolis, Maryland, where its offices remain today, the Naval Institute has members worldwide.

Members of the Naval Institute support the education programs of the society and receive the influential monthly magazine *Proceedings* and discounts on fine nautical prints and on ship and aircraft photos. They also have access to the transcripts of the Institute's Oral History Program and get discounted admission to any of the Institute-sponsored seminars offered around the country. Discounts are also available to the colorful bimonthly magazine *Naval History*.

The Naval Institute's book-publishing program, begun in 1898 with basic guides to naval practices, has broadened its scope to include books of more general interest. Now the Naval Institute Press publishes about seventy titles each year, ranging from how-to books on boating and navigation to battle histories, biographies, ship and aircraft guides, and novels. Institute members receive significant discounts on the Press's more than eight hundred books in print.

Full-time students are eligible for special half-price membership rates. Life memberships are also available.

For a free catalog describing Naval Institute Press books currently available, and for further information about joining the U.S. Naval Institute, please write to:

Member Services
U.S. NAVAL INSTITUTE
291 Wood Road
Annapolis, MD 21402-5034
Telephone: 800-233-8764
Fax: 410-571-1703
Web address: *www.navalinstitute.org*